The Normal Accident Theory
of Education

The Normal Accident Theory
of Education

Why Reform and Regulation Won't Make Schools Better

Andrew K. Milton

ROWMAN & LITTLEFIELD
Lanham • Boulder • New York • Toronto • Plymouth, UK

Published by Rowman & Littlefield
4501 Forbes Boulevard, Suite 200, Lanham, Maryland 20706
www.rowman.com

10 Thornbury Road, Plymouth PL6 7PP, United Kingdom

British Library Cataloguing in Publication Information Available

Library of Congress Cataloging-in-Publication Data

Library of Congress Cataloging-in-Publication Data Available

ISBN 978-1-4758-0657-1 (cloth : alk. paper) -- ISBN 978-1-4758-0658-8 (pbk. : alk. paper) -- ISBN 978-1-4758-0659-5 (electronic)

∞™ The paper used in this publication meets the minimum requirements of American National Standard for Information Sciences Permanence of Paper for Printed Library Materials, ANSI/NISO Z39.48-1992.

Printed in the United States of America

Contents

Acknowledgments

I am indebted to many people, without whose help and encouragement this book would never have been conceived or written. It seemed more than ironic (normal serendipity?) that Charles Perrow, whose ideas about normal accidents form the conceptual backbone of this work, also hailed from Tacoma (he in the past, I presently), so, noting that, I wrote to thank him for his work. In his generosity he thanked *me* for finding the normal accident idea useful, especially in a field "I know little about. . . . I am delighted if normal accident theory can be useful even in education," he said.

Several others read and commented on—either in part or whole—early drafts of the book. Patrick O'Neil, of the University of Puget Sound, and I have shared twenty years of a consistently fruitful scholarly friendship. In that time he has pondered, studied, written about, and taught on almost all of the topics I've ever known or studied (including normal accidents), so it was natural that I should ask him to review this work. His comments, responses, and advice were essential.

Walt Gardner, author of the Reality Check blog on education, helped me more sharply identify the book's audience and shape the words that would reach them. Richard Anderson, of the Puget Sound Partnership, introduced me to the structured decision-making ideas. Greg Pierce, a public policy specialist in another field, but an impressively omnivorous intellect, also gave me important feedback on early drafts. Liv Finne, director of the Center for Education at the Washington Policy Center, encouraged me in the work, noting the importance of the message in the material.

Several teachers and other education staff read some or all of the manuscript. Michael Jankanish, an AP civics teacher with the highest reputation, enriched my teacher's perspective. Walt Erhardt, Margaret Kirn, Ken Richardson, Dick Hannula, and Derek Beaulieu likewise added to the work.

Tom Koerner and Carlie Wall, at Rowman & Littlefield, were invaluable. They patiently answered my questions—too often delivered by way of incomplete serial e-mails—about every detail of the process.

Sandy, my wife, did more than I had right to ask. From listening—repeatedly—to me work out the logic and details of the book's arguments and examples to proofreading various drafts, she enthusiastically supported the work that has become this book.

Finally, my father, Kent Milton—who has spent the last sixty-odd years writing articles, speeches, studies, press releases, and more—contributed mightily to this work. I am grateful both that he passed his writing gene on to me and that he modeled delight in the writing process. Lacking either one of these, I would never have undertaken this work.

Tacoma, WA
January 2014

Preface

I have been teaching eighth grade language arts (what we called English, when I was in eighth grade) in a public school near Tacoma, Washington, for eight years. In that time, I've seen a variety of educational reforms (fads, depending on who you ask or on how the new idea was presented) come along. Once they've come, though, they only go as far as educators adjust or adapt or disregard them, especially as they fit or not with the next round of the latest and greatest "research-based best practices." In other words, each round of reform leaves a residual imprint of expectations and guidelines upon which school staff must implement subsequent reform plans. Each time, the slate gets dustier with the remnants of the chalk from the previous ideas and programs.

This year, for instance, Washington state teachers are spending their second or third year gearing up for the "rollout" (a seemingly ubiquitous word) of the new Common Core State Standards, due to be officially in place by the 2014–2015 school year (in Washington state) *and*, at the same time, learning the details of a completely redesigned teacher evaluation system, on which I and several other district staff members spent nearly five days training.

As I write, however, the federal Department of Education has officially notified Washington that this new plan for incorporating student learning into teacher evaluations does not meet federal expectations. With only days until school starts, it remains unclear just what the new teacher evaluation process will actually look like. Never mind, though . . . teachers will carry on with their work next week.

In short, education is undergoing nearly constant reform, but in far too many ways the process of change is incomprehensible to many of the people responsible for implementing those changes. As new program piles upon new restructuring, the "system" grows increasingly unwieldy for those who are charged with running a classroom every day.

This persistent change, erratically ordered as it is, tends to generate a hulking and confusing educational "system" and bureaucracy whose mandates, with their attendant quirks, flow downward to class room teachers responsible for implementing them. The machinery gear images below are an astoundingly awkward and comic metaphor for this situation. Further, they illustrate the very logic that underwrites the main argument of this book.

To think of the comic aspect, try to remember the number of times you've heard people complain about how education has become like a machine, cranking out mere workers with which to feed an insatiable economic beast. Even the recent *Waiting for Superman* uses this visual image when depicting how fifty years ago the less academically minded students would step straight into good factory jobs.

One important part of that film's demands for education reform is based on the fact that this route is so much less available today. Indeed, we are talking about jobs, job skills, economic competitiveness, and so on to eighth graders in my district. In other words, we are alarmed to think of education machinery cranking out the human industrial "parts," but we teach about work and jobs ever earlier in the educational trajectory.

Another depressingly comedic aspect of the gear metaphor is that many people feel themselves a cog ground down by the gears of an education machine. You don't have to have seen *Modern Times* to know and understand the image of Chaplin's factory worker getting caught in the wheels of a system much bigger and more powerful than he is. Teachers and staff sometimes feel this way, but so, too, do students and parents, who can occasionally feel like they face gears turning in directions opposite to what they prefer or value.

Finally, look closely at each image. In the first, students do not even make an appearance. A crank called the "anchor standards" drives what teachers do in all the sub-disciplinary elements of language arts. But this machine lacks a place for students, so what it produces ultimately remains unclear.

The second gear arrangement has its own oddity. It seems that the effective functioning of those gears has no connection to student learning. As the cogs in the machine turn, they have no apparent effect on what we assume to be the primary rationale for creating this machine in the first place. Without gear teeth at "student learning," this piece of the machinery will sit, inert, even while the rest of the machine hums along.

Students are part of the third machinery, but if relative size indicates anything, they are much less relevant than all the adult staff of the school district. Furthermore, district administrators apparently have a direct impact on students, but not on teachers. Even in small districts, this is hard to imagine. This image is no doubt intended to convey the collaborative nature

College and Career Readiness Machinery. Source: ReadTennessee.org.

of the education project, but the teacher has much more significance in the students' lives than do district administrators, so this image misleads in some degree.

More importantly for this book, without realizing, the creators of these images have provided perfect visual metaphors for the main argument proffered here. Schools, being bureaucratic structures, conceive and execute education in ways shaped and bounded by their organizational realities. One of those realities is that complex and tightly bound systems can be expected to fail—have accidents—as a function of their complexity and tightness. This is most easily seen in technological systems, like a nuclear reactor or an airplane, but we will apply the logic to bureaucratic systems, too.

The key insight of the theory, originating in the work of sociologist Charles Perrow, is that these normal accidents are not caused by design flaw or operator error. Rather, the system's tightness raises the consequence of small errors or malfunctions, as these pass quickly to other parts of the system. Complexity makes the monitoring, observation, and correcting of

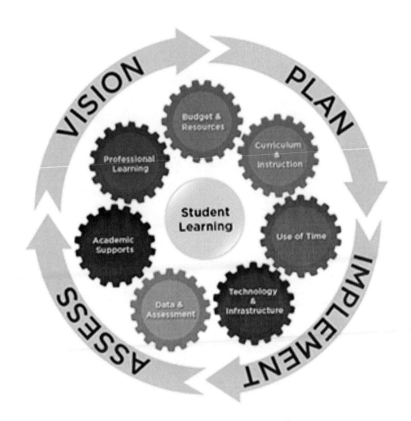

Student Learning Machinery. Source: Alliance for Excellent Education, "Project 24 Framework," http://www.digitallearningday.org/partners/project-24/gears/ (accessed August 27, 2013).

these malfunctions more difficult, occasionally—but predictably—generating a few "we figured it out too late" failures.

As I told colleagues about the ideas I am trying to use in this book (before discovering the gear images presented here), I usually summarized normal accidents by talking about systems with gears, while simultaneously making the typical depiction using fingers of both hands, interlocked and "cranking" like a set of gears. Rather than make these goofy and abstruse gestures, now I just send them the images in this preface.

The potency of the visual metaphor—both my hands and these images—goes halfway to convincing me that "I'm onto something" with these ideas. But education is a multitudinous business, sloppy and repetitive. Machinery gears, drawing on the archetypical image of the mechanical clockworks, evoke a picture of consistent and constant execution of the same action over and over—thus the expression "like clockwork."

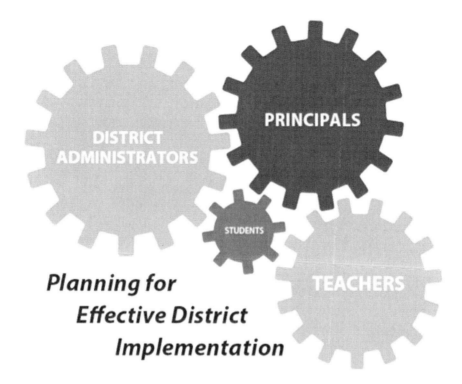

Implementation Machinery. Source: Education Northwest.

To the contrary, education is repetitive—skills and ideas are covered myriad times in a student's career; but, this is best accomplished when variation is added to presentation, lest students lose interest and/or learn skills in narrow and specific circumstances. In other words, education is nothing like clockwork.

Yet, schools are large bureaucratic organizations, which means they follow certain sets of protocols, and seek to maximize their performance by getting good at a set of procedures which they effectively repeat with each new batch of students. So, when we face the fact that *varied individuals*, with disparate and sometimes divergent hopes and goals, enter a *bureaucratic organization*, possessed of far fewer sets of procedures than there are students, to get something we call *an education*, the preferred content of which is subject to significant debate and disagreement, we must admit of complexity and complication.

Describing, evaluating, and addressing that complexity is the purpose of this book. Obviously, I do not know every situation as thoroughly as I know my own, which means that much of this book is based on my direct experiences, or my analytical response to issues and circumstances about which I read.

In many ways that is the point of this book—different districts, different schools, even different class room teachers will experience and respond differently to the complex system in which we all work. Like most teachers, I've had conversations with teachers from numerous school districts, I've read books and articles about other teachers' experiences, and I've even done several informal surveys of teacher attitudes about a variety of issues.

I write, then, with the hope of providing a "teacher's-eye view" of schools, teaching, and learning. At the same time, I will filter this material through the lens of a social science approach to organizations and bureaucracy. The thoughts, ideas, claims, and so on offered here are something of a hybrid of these, my two professional backgrounds—academic social scientist and education professional. Likely, "specialists" from both areas will find inadequate the work based on that element wherein lies their own experience. And so it probably is, but all the better, as I suspect that neither side—even in its academic "depth"—by itself gets as rich a picture as the hybrid rendered here.

If you are a parent reading this book, I hope you will gain a more supple understanding of some of the vagaries of your local school, and feel more competent and confident to speak with your school staff about your children's education. If you are a teacher, I hope you will feel some encouragement that while the "system" is daunting and even vexing, you can still do good work with your students. Finally, if you are an education bureaucrat or reformer, I hope you will take heed that schools are idiosyncratic, so local insight and wisdom can add significant value to the process of changing education. For whatever reason you are reading this, I hope you enjoy it.

Chapter One

The Problem with Public Schools

This introductory overview reviews the life and circumstances of a composite student—the Johnny of *Why Johnny Can't Read* from all the way back in 1955. The organizational opportunities and constraints derived from the particular institutional structure of schools are introduced.

The very titles of both this chapter and the book probably initiate the sharpening of the intellectual, and perhaps polemical, knives. For those predisposed against the public schools—either for their expense, their supposed decaying effectiveness, or their increasingly dubious social role—the thinking probably goes something like, "Problem with the public schools? There's only one?" or, "Right, schools are normally accidents . . . train wrecks, that is."

On the other hand, those who tend to support or like the schools (or at least the one their children attend) might respond, "What's the use of another laundry list of failures in the schools?" And for those who work in the schools, it might be both, with the addition of, "How many Gates Foundation studies does it take to blame teachers for every ill in society?"

Forgive the conceit, for conceit it is. "The murky muddled situation in the public schools" seems unlikely to stir as much enthusiasm or grab the attention. But that is precisely the situation the schools find themselves in. And this muddled middle creates plenty of fuel for both sides of the polarized discussion, so stark claims and dramatic conclusions abound. Our civic discussion about schools would immeasurably improve if everyone engaged in that conversation slowed down and took a more thorough look at the schools, students, families, staff, and the general institutional and cultural circumstances of the relationship among all these people.

Upon entering into this discussion first note that schools are bureaucratic organizations which work with individuals . . . lots of them. As bureaucracies are wont to do, schools and school districts are organized and oriented around patterns, routines, and procedures. The 500, 1,000, or 2,000 students in a school, however, constitute a wide variety of individual needs, hopes, expectations, and capacities.

Schools as bureaucratic organizations find themselves in the awkward position of trying to create more procedures so they can address the disparate needs of their own student population. Individual students, meanwhile, must navigate an increasingly complicated and convoluted organization in order to meet their educational needs and requirements.

This book describes and evaluates the consequences of this disjuncture between schools as organizations and students as individuals. The main objective is to describe, explain, and evaluate this situation, in which schools undertake the responsibility to make Johnny read, make Jane ready for her virtuoso career in whatever she chooses, and everything in between, as the last social institution standing.

A visit with a current Johnny, descended from the famous Johnny of *Why Johnny Can't Read*[1] fame, gives us the first view of the difficulties arising from this organizational disconnect. A substantial portion of the current claims that schools aren't working rests, after all, on the persistent presence of an unacceptably high number of students who fail to meet standards (expectations for their age, so to speak). Consequently, much, though not all, of the focus of reform revolves around how to get these children back up to the academic standards for their age. Thus the explanation of why Johnny still can't read today.

Rudolf Flesch first introduced Johnny to the world in 1955 and claimed he couldn't read because he was being taught wrongly. Memorizing sight words doesn't help Johnny figure out (decode) new words when he encounters them, Flesch pointed out, so we needed to go back to phonics (understanding phonemic relationships of letters). Easy enough, so it seems. But the supposed persistence of reading deficiencies today means that either Flesch was wrong (he wasn't—phonics-like decoding is necessary for new words, which eventually do become sight words . . . after reading them often enough), or nobody listened to Flesch (many did, and got caught up in highly emotional pedagogical debates), or something else is going on.

So, what do we know now about Johnny and his reading? Suppose Johnny is about to enter middle school, sixth grade, and he is already several years behind grade level in reading. Perhaps the easiest way to figure out why is to work backward Johnny's last several years, starting with that first day in sixth grade.

The first task is to determine the precise nature of Johnny's reading "problems." If he has phonemic awareness difficulties (doesn't know his letter sounds), he can't decode words as he reads them, and he will quit reading within a few minutes of starting, for he will quickly struggle with what are basic words for strong readers. Imagine قراءة this sentence when 당신 really can't make out all the речи because εσείς don't دانستن enough of the letters to even انداز ہ~ـ at the word, let alone its 意味. (Imagine reading this sentence when you really can't figure out all the words because you don't know enough of the letters to even guess at the word, let alone its meaning. Chances are, though, that if you're reading this, you're a strong enough reader to actually guess at that sentence, but it was a lot more work than regular reading.)

The mechanics of reading, using phonemic awareness, are only the beginning of the potential difficulties Johnny might have, though. Problems with what is too broadly called "understanding what he reads" may still persist, even if his reading mechanics are strong. Johnny may read with reasonable fluency (identify and pronounce the words well) but have a comprehension weakness, which allows Johnny to read but without really knowing what he's reading. These are, of course, two different kinds of problems, requiring different intervention responses.

Johnny really needs to spend some time getting extra repetitions (just like exercise, strengthening your reading requires practice and repetition). At school, he probably needs a class where readers at comparable levels can work on the same types of skill deficiencies. Without an intervention, and left in a general language arts or English class, Johnny will read less successfully than the students who are reading grade-level material, and will likely withdraw, intellectually, from the class (though he may desire to remain socially engaged, which can end up in general class room disruption as he tries to socialize about things other than the class material). He will probably remain frustrated with reading, and he will not get that extra practice he so desperately needs.

Interventions are available for Johnny. Intensive programs of practice have been shown to get two years (or more) reading growth in one school year. Forty years of successful intervention seems compelling, but in the case of the so-called direct instruction programs (which are highly scripted), many teachers reject the program in deference to their own pedagogical values, their distaste for boring curriculum or their gut feeling that the program "just isn't right."

Even so, many districts use such programs to great effect. So, why would Johnny fall so far behind so fast? Well, for a variety of reasons. Johnny may have indeed had a reading intervention in an earlier grade, but perhaps he moved and the new district didn't have an intervention program, or anything in the same style and format. The demands for local control over schools, which have left us with nearly 15,000 independent school-governing bodies, means that incoherence from district to district is not only possible, but unavoidable. Partly for this reason (as well as others), frequent moving can have a deleterious effect on academic performance.

Similarly, Johnny might have a significant absenteeism issue. Plenty of struggling students do exhibit more absences than average, creating a vicious cycle of underdeveloped skills that lead to less interest which increases the desire to stay away from school. Reading intervention programs, though, are intensive and highly structured, and therefore require consistent participation.

Suppose Johnny does consistently go to his reading intervention class and his general education English class, and begins to show gains . . . then he moves. Moving to a new district, even if done seamlessly (which is unlikely—the social-psychological effects of moving are usually at least somewhat negative), can disrupt the intervention gains, as Johnny gets evaluated, placed, socialized, and so forth in the new district. It will be even harder for Johnny if his new district uses a different remediation program or system, as his earlier gains wouldn't be as smoothly built upon as if he'd stayed in place. And if Johnny moves to a different state, the organizational confusion mounts even higher.

Johnny doesn't have to move, though, for his situation to worsen. If Johnny's school district suffered budget cutbacks significant enough, the school leadership probably had to make choices about which programs to keep and which to cut. The choice is not an easy one, as sometimes it can look like choosing to help one group of students instead of another, but in the end his district might have cut back on the particular reading intervention he needed.

Or maybe Johnny really did have a string of bad teachers—men and women who neglected him, or whole groups of youngsters, and let the reading basics just slip by. This explanation seems among the more popular at the moment. Gates Foundation studies, stirring documentaries, and teacher performance incentive contracts all put the onus for Johnny's difficulties on teachers.

Fine enough, teachers should be accountable for their performance. But in the current social climate, teachers and schools are uniquely responsible for Johnny's failure to read. Parents and students are treated as neutral (or even active but frustrated by the school's ineptness) in this story, passive recipients of reading services from the schools. But to be successful at learning to read, Johnny and his parents need to be active, not passive. A closer look at Johnny's situation will show how.

We know—from common sense as well as studies—that parents who read are more likely to raise children who read, and parents who don't, won't. Shirley Brice Heath's classic study[2] revealed the intimate details of how this replication process works. The institution of the school has no social mechanism available, however, to hold parents to the expectation that they prepare their children for reading, or for school more generally. So, if Johnny's parents do not make reading important by reading to him, and maybe—just maybe—teaching him the ABC song, and a few letter names before he shows up at kindergarten, he's already behind.

Indeed, ask a kindergarten teacher about the ability to predict which students will struggle deep into their school careers. It's a prophecy written before the first day of school, and fulfilled by parents who didn't and don't read to Johnny. We will learn in a later chapter how wrong early teachers' assessments can be, and the social and organizational reasons for these errors,[3] but the point remains that once Johnny is delivered to the schoolhouse door, teachers and the schools will be held singularly responsible for the outcome, and, subsequently, for making Johnny read.

In response to Johnny's difficulties, the schools try to devise reading intervention programs to address Johnny's needs. But even an effective intervention program needs to be reinforced throughout other areas of the student's life, particularly at home. David Brooks reported in the *New York Times*[4] on studies that confirmed what many people assert from intuition, namely, that a summer reading program (of just twelve books, as it turns out) not only stems the "summer drop-off" so prevalent in struggling students, but actually improves their academic performance and testing.

We also know, of course, that struggling students are precisely the ones least likely to read twelve books over the summer. They are struggling because they don't read well. They don't enjoy reading since they're not strong at it, so they don't read, and they suffer the summer drop-off, falling back even further, and on it goes. This downward spiral can be reversed, of course, but it would take intentional and intensive work at school, at home, and during the summer—intentional effort by teachers and parents, but most of all Johnny.

So we, as a community, are left with something of a mess. When Johnny falls behind in reading, and the school is the primary instrument of closing that gap, it will be an uphill battle. The situation would improve dramatically if Johnny were invested in the work. But if he's not—and all too often he's not, since his interest drops as his skills diminish further—then the task for the school is all the more daunting. Organizational and institutional exigencies reveal why.

Suppose Johnny gets two daily classes (one regular language class and one intervention class) devoted to reading work all year. His school will have focused work time equivalent to two full weeks—roughly 340 hours—on Johnny's reading. If Malcolm Gladwell's claims about needing 10,000 hours of practice to achieve virtuosity[5] are even half right, it takes at least several thousand hours—spread out over years—to master and sustain even high-level reading skills, the kind that involve analysis, interpretation, prediction, inference, response, and so forth.

Even if Johnny had the "double dip" of reading classes for the remaining seven years of his academic career, that amounts to less than 2,400 hours (provided he's never absent), all of which would not be completely devoted solely to his reading practice—there are other students in the class, after all. Clearly, any remediation of basic skills by the school really requires that Johnny continue to practice at home.

To hope for even those 2,400 hours in school is a pipe dream, though. The schools just don't have the personnel available to offer the small classes that allow the greater repetitions Johnny needs. When general education class size maximums are thirty-two, and remediation program requirements (according to the curriculum's producers) call for classes of twelve to fifteen, the numbers just won't pencil. Johnny might get one or two years of double classes, but after that he's likely back into the general language arts classes.

He's particularly unlikely to get much remediation in high school . . . it's just too late. Most mainstream comprehensive high schools focus more on credit retrieval than remediation, because the marginal benefit of such late intervention is negligible, and the high school's performance is based on graduation rate as much as skills development.

Add to this the awkward and confusing state and federal rules, tied, of course, to the money they each dangle before school districts. Sometimes the regulatory directives can undermine an individual school's intervention efforts. Some programs of support, which might be funded by specific government regulations, require Johnny to qualify for that program. If Johnny really needs intervention, but doesn't qualify for the particular program, which might be the primary intervention that district has opted (or is compelled by law) to undertake, he might just end up in a general language arts class only—about 170 hours a year, with 32 students, and many fewer extra repetitions.

If Johnny does get some extra help, it might be in the Learning Assistance Program (LAP) (from Title I of the Elementary and Secondary Education Act, popularly called No Child Left Behind), a federal program that grants money to state education bureaucracies, which disburse that money to school districts based on the low-income (the "free and reduced lunch") population of the school. The district then distributes the money to individual schools who hire extra teachers to run smaller classes for the most educationally needy students. The individual school gets to determine the criteria for placing kids in these LAP classes.

But suppose Johnny is at a middle school of 700 students, in a solidly middle class district (say, 20 percent free and reduced lunch). The district distributes its Title I funds such that Johnny's school gets one LAP teacher, who has five classes of eight to ten students. That would be five classes for all of the sixth, seventh, and eighth graders, for language and math. The school has to make a decision about whom to serve—which grade levels, which subjects.

One option is to simply choose not to do one grade level of one subject, say eighth grade reading. So if Johnny needs some extra help in reading, and his school has opted not to have a LAP class for what he needs, and he doesn't qualify for special education, then he doesn't get any extra help. Unless, of course, the school offers a reading skills class, out of its own pocket—that is, it uses one class period of a general education teacher's day for the class. This would mean, of course, that the other general education teachers would have to accept larger classes during the time their colleague had only twelve students instead of thirty. All this is organizationally difficult to create and sustain.

Johnny has a problem, indeed. The schools may be part of that problem. The schools are undoubtedly part of the solution, but only part. For the schools are an institution in a broader society that, frankly, is showing some educational erosion. Plenty of social conditions that have nothing to do with schools or the reading curriculum contribute substantially to Johnny's academic struggles.

Plenty of these conditions have roots reaching all the way back to the original Johnny of the 1950s. For instance, female labor force participation began its long steady climb more than fifty years ago. This meant that mothers, or even extended family relatives, were less available to be reading (or overseeing school work, generally) as much with Johnny. Further, suburbanization, with its longer commutes, also meant fathers had less time at home. Finally, we lament the effects of too much "screen time" today, but, of course, the long march to this unfortunate circumstance began with television, in the 1950s.[6]

Screen time is arguably the biggest problem for Johnny. If he's average, he engages in about seven hours of TV watching, computer gazing, and video game playing *each day*.[7] That means he spends more time in non-reading screen activities each day than he does in language arts class all week. Every year, he will get about as many hours in screen time as he would in the seven more years of double dip reading classes. Of course, Johnny is quite likely the kind of youngster who drives the screen time average as high as it is, so the numbers might actually be worse.

Screen time isn't just lost intellectual time either. The growing insights into brain physiology and chemistry continue to reveal that excessive screen time affects brain development in ways that are not conducive to reading or academic engagement generally. Moreover, such extensive periods of physical inactivity have hormonal effects that can also make attention and focus—on something like reading—more difficult.[8]

Technology generates some educational benefits—access to more material, some enriched support opportunities—but the point here is that the process of helping a struggling student (a) is very different from helping a student who is performing at grade level, (b) can be an organizationally and pedagogically daunting task for individual schools, and (c) reflects the kind of social and institutional strain schools live with. For Johnny's story does highlight something of the mess schools are in.

This is not to say schools are a mess—rather they are in a messy spot. Education is a sloppily expensive proposition. We have to repeat the same things for each year's new group of students, and do so for every student. As an organizational structure the school strains under growing regulatory and programmatic demands, all of which make it more difficult to address the increasingly divergent educational needs of a student population with widely disparate readiness and skill levels. The broadening and tightening of regulations and expectations increase the complexity of meeting these diverse and divergent needs.

Further, as the network of institutions and order keepers (even the family) has crumbled in our society, schools are, in fact, called upon as something of the last best chance for some kids. At the extremes, some students get free breakfast and lunch at school, get referrals for some kinds of medical care, and spend after school hours in school-related programs. Some principals have even gone so far as to go to the homes of absent students and bring them to school. Not to put too fine a point on it, but schools work better than a lot of other social institutions and so, in fact, are being called upon to do ever more. A few stories will illustrate this.

Every teacher has had plenty of students whose parents don't respond to e-mails and phone calls about Johnny and not why he can't read, but why he won't do any number of things he is capable of doing, like putting his name on a piece of work and handing it in after just having completed it along with the rest of the class only moments before. It doesn't take a research study to see that such parental unresponsiveness tends to correlate with poor student performance, from homework to the standardized tests.

Or think of the host of new responsibilities falling to schools when the institution of the family steps aside in this kind of way. For instance, every school has its fair share of the cyberbullying episodes like this: parents of a teenage girl find lewd text messages from another student on their daughter's phone, and then ask the school principal to investigate and address the case, even though the offending activities were undertaken outside of school time and off school grounds.

In one case reported in the *New York Times*,[9] it seems the offended father felt uncomfortable approaching the other father because he knew him socially. Time was this would be an ideal opportunity for the two fathers to "get to the bottom" of the situation. Now, the school is beseeched to help, and at great risk. Imagine what would happen if the school finds differently from what the offended parent expects or hopes.

Speaking of technology, the television is the oldest, but not the most insidious, gadget to corrode the family. As more and more gadgets offer private and individual entertainments and distractions, students spend more and more time in an electronic world of their own making—and with less and less parental oversight, a world much more pleasing than doing school work.

Every teacher has had plenty of students report, as if it was a great and good thing (and why wouldn't they, nobody or nothing tells them it's not), that they have their own TV, often with a game unit, and their own computer in their bedroom. Add the ever-present cell phone, and it's not hard to see how the practice of reading or math or any other school activity loses the competition for a youngster's attention.

Don't miss, by the way, the irony of schools giving students family-corroding laptops that contribute to this electronic distraction and make the educational process more complicated. But what else could schools do? In a society infatuated with technology, and convinced that technological solutions will always be good and helpful, schools have to cover themselves by getting more of the electronic salvation supposedly available in the latest device.

Having more computers indicates the school's commitment to doing everything possible to educate Johnny and his peers. Foregoing computers is construed as derelict—a technological stone left unturned. You don't have to strain to hear the questions that would arise. "Why isn't the school getting more computers?" To say, "Because they're not good for education" would simply sound nonsensical in a culture so enthralled by the latest gadgets, devices, and apps.

Schools are also in a messy spot to the extent that they are charged with "educating the whole child" while they are assessed by the number of students who pass annual tests in reading, writing, math, and science. This is not to say that standardized tests are intrinsically bad, or that schools needn't face some measure of accountability. But rendering proof of a school's meeting its responsibility to the whole child by way of a few test scores is incomplete, inadequate, and probably misleading.

Even so, some school reformers gush over the plans (of the type undertaken most famously by Michelle Rhee before she departed her post superintending the Washington, DC, schools) to develop a scoring system for teachers, so they can evaluate performance. To the extent this scoring will be based on the standardized test score outcomes of their students, teachers, being no less rational than the general population, will respond to the incentives before them, and find it harder to resist "teaching to the test." It doesn't take much imagination to see the Gates Foundation studies a few years from now: "Teachers aren't as 'effective' as they seem—too many just teach to the test."

Frankly, the heavy emphasis on the test already creates a great temptation to teach to the test, especially because the gold ring is merely a high, or at least increasing, pass rate. In other words, if a teacher could get 100 percent of his/her students to pass the state test, even if they all achieved the minimum passing score, while some showed significant decrease from their prior scores, that teacher would be garlanded with glory for the remarkable achievement of a perfect pass rate.

By contrast, imagine a teacher whose students all missed the standard by only one point. Further imagine that teacher got a substantial number of students to make significant gains in score, though just short of passing. This teacher would not be heralded in the newspaper or on the district web site or anywhere else.

It's just too much to explain that while everybody failed, most made really great growth. But the political and reform winds are blowing into a perfect storm in which these test scores will carry increasing weight in the discussion of evaluating teachers and schools. Practically every teacher in service now starts with the requisite hand-wringing over the United States's pitiful rankings in international test score comparisons, where we're falling behind the likes of Latvia and Spain and so many others.

The situation may not be as dramatic as has been made to seem, though. Stephen Krashen, an independent analyst and scholar of education, finds that when controlling for socio-economic status, the American students' scores on the international reading tests place the United States in the top quartile of similarly developed countries. [10]

But seriously evaluating these many complicated situations is just too awkward. It's too awkward to raise questions about the standard—how it's set, for what purpose—to the neglect of what other values (there are no tests for right conduct and attitude, in part, of course, because nobody wants to discuss what these might look like), or about parental responsibility in children's education, or about students' responsibilities to their own education. And it's too awkward to point out that education really is a socially costly undertaking. The most awkward of all is thinking about the ways that some schools are, in fact, doing remarkable things under pretty demanding circumstances.

What's the score, then, when schools do some things well and others things quite poorly? Sweeping sociological claims about what schools are like and what they should do are difficult to make, yet analysts, experts, and reformers do this routinely. The rest of this book will try, then, to explain why some things work in schools while others don't, why there are still so many Johnnies at the same time that school has gotten much more rigorous in many ways, and why some schools thrive and others fail.

In this chapter, we took a snapshot of the social and organizational challenges that schools face. In an environment of heightening expectations, corroding social institutions and stifling bureaucratic requirements, schools (and staff) are called on for so much—academically, socially, morally, and more. We continue our walk through the woods of American schools by examining the odd and counterintuitive idea that complex organizations or systems routinely fail, sometimes catastrophically.

The next chapter explains the source of this routine failure—an organizational reality called "normal accidents," and explains how the increasing complexity of schools is not well fit to the complex systems that are children's brains. Following that, we move on to examine how the social culture and organizational circumstances of schools make failure more likely by creating unreasonable expectations for schools and teachers.

Next comes an explanation of how the standardized test process makes this normal failure more likely by masking the very prospect and presence of that failure. Following this is an explanation of the weakness of connecting teacher evaluations to standardized tests. From there we will consider the ways technology adds complexity to schools. After this we review the ways that market logic and analogy fail when applied to schools. Finally, given all this normal failure, we will consider some "next steps," as the education world aficionados are wont to say.

NOTES

1. Rudolf Flesch, *Why Johnny Can't Read—And What You Can Do About It* (New York: Harper & Row, 1955). Reissued, 1986.

2. Shirley Brice Heath, "What No Bedtime Story Means: Narrative Skills at Home and School," *Language in Society*, 11, no. 1 (1982): 49-76.

3. Po Bronson and Ashley Merryman, *NurtureShock: New Thinking About Children* (New York: Twelve, 2009), chap. 2.

4. David Brooks, "The Medium is the Medium," *New York Times*, July 8, 2010. http://www.nytimes.com/2010/07/09/opinion/09brooks.html?_r=4&.

5. Malcolm Gladwell, *Outliers: The Story of Success* (New York: Little, Brown & Co., 2008), chap. 1.

6. Robert Putnam, *Bowling Alone: The Collapse and Revival of American Community* (New York: Simon & Schuster, 2001), chap. 13.

7. "Generation M2: Media in the Lives of 8- to 18-Year-Olds," Kaiser Family Foundation, January 20, 2010.

8. John Medina, *Brain Rules: 12 Principles for Surviving and Thriving at Work, Home, and School* (Seattle: Pear Press, 2008), chap. 1.

9. Jan Hoffman, "Online Bullies Pull Schools Into the Fray," *New York Times*, June 27, 2010. http://www.nytimes.com/2010/06/28/style/28bully.html?pagewanted=all.

10. Diane Ravitch, "Stephen Krashen: Our PISA Scores are Just Right," *Diane Ravitch's Blog* (blog), December 9, 2012, http://dianeravitch.net/2012/12/09/stephen-krashen-our-pisa-scores-are-just-right/.

Chapter Two

Why Schools Have Normal Accidents Routinely

This conceptual chapter reviews the normal accident theory and applies it to schools and brains. Schools have traditionally been complex but loosely coupled organizations (many interworking parts but with slack in the system). Well-functioning brains are also highly complex and need a wide variety of inputs to develop rightly.

In this chapter I argue that the organizational tightening that follows from greater regulation of schools (No Child Left Behind, for instance) actually increases the probability of normal accidents because the slack that allows for stopping to fix failures has been taken out of the system. Furthermore, by narrowing the measures of performance—test results—we enable ourselves to ignore educational failures that are not discerned by the test outcomes.

Education, both as an individual activity and as a social process, is a complicated, expensive, and sloppy endeavor. The institutions that undertake to educate youngsters are effective and productive in some ways, and ineffective in others. Public, private, vouchered, charter schools—even parents at home—all evoke this variability, though in different ways. This is so because, being a complicated undertaking, education is susceptible to normal accidents.

The near meltdown of the core in a nuclear power plant thirty-five years ago will help us understand why education has many of the issues and weaknesses that it does. Analyzing the Three Mile Island episode, Charles Perrow explained why we should expect what he called normal accidents in systems characterized by two critical features—interactive complexity of a system's parts, and tightness of the coupling among the component parts. [1]

13

A system is composed of various parts whose relationship is characterized by some degree of complexity. An interactively complex system has
many component elements and/or processes that are connected in such a way
that each element's performance is vital, because the effective interactions
among all the component elements are necessary for proper functioning of
the whole system.

Complex, as opposed to linear, systems are characterized by simultaneous
processes within the system, where these processes affect other elements of
the system. The degree of looseness or tightness of the coupling—or connection—of these parts reflects the system's slack, the ability to absorb problems
without failing. Complex systems and tight systems evoke some risk of normal accidents, while systems that are both complex and tight carry the greatest likelihood of normal accidents.

The visual analogy of the gear-driven machine from the preface illustrates
the point. Since all the gears are tightly connected together and both driven
by and driving other gears, a failure in any part of the works will quickly
result in system-wide malfunction. The increased complexity makes it more
difficult to discern the malfunction before it ripples throughout the whole
system, resulting in failure on a grander scale . . . and failure that we should
come to expect as a matter of course in complex and tightly bound systems.

This likelihood of routine failure reaches such heights because it is precisely when system elements are tightly bound that any mistake in the interaction of those parts will ratchet through the whole system quickly. When the
connections among system parts are complex, errors—which are passing
quickly through the system—and their sources become more difficult to
observe and monitor. The quickly spreading but hard to see problem sometimes creates catastrophic system failure that operators and observers fail to
understand "before it's too late."

Perrow calls these *normal accidents* in order to emphasize that we should
expect a certain amount of failure in such systems. Further, these normal or
inevitable accidents are not the result of design flaw or operator error. Instead, they arise out of predictable and routine small failures in a system
whose complexity makes it difficult to discern the failure while it is still
manageable. In other words, every so often complex tightly coupled systems
will fail, as a predictable result of their tight complexity.

Perrow wrote his seminal work on normal accidents in the years following the near meltdown of the nuclear reactor at Three Mile Island in Pennsyl-
vania in 1979. For this reason, he elaborates extensively on nuclear power
plants as the quintessential tightly coupled complex system. (See the upper
right corner of Figure 2.1, reproduced from his book.)

He was particularly concerned with systems whose normal accidents have
catastrophic results, the way a nuclear meltdown would, or, on a narrower
scale, the way the O-ring failure on the Challenger booster rocket did in

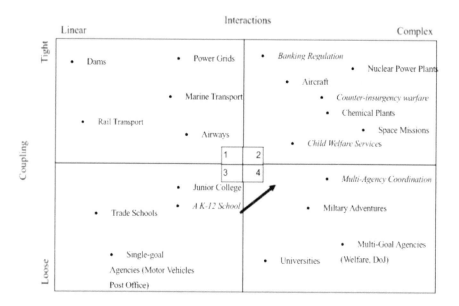

Figure 2.1.   Italicized items are 2013 additions. K-12 schools are moving from less to more complex, and from loose to tighter (see arrow). Source: Author, based on Charles Perrow, 1984, chap. 3.

1986.[2] Normal accidents also occur in more prosaic environments, even ones in which we are somewhat accustomed to accidents that do result from design or operator error. For instance, William Langewiesche relied on normal accident reasoning to explain with great clarity how the organizational complexity of oxygen canister management at the handling facility set in motion the events that led to Valujet 592 falling into the Florida Everglades in 1996.[3]

Professor Dick Piccard of Ohio University has created an overview[4]— both thorough and accessible—of Perrow's normal accident theory, in which he summarized several key terms that constitute the general idea. Piccard's summary (highlighted in the table below) allows some general conceptual analysis of the ways that schools and the "school system" are prone to normal accidents. Drawing on this summary, we can get a basic introduction to some of the issues that later chapters will cover more thoroughly.

Other systems' normal accidents have less obviously catastrophic failure, like those in the lower left cell (#3) in the figure above. For instance, Perrow says that universities are loosely coupled complex systems. The operation of the various and multiple bureaucracies is complex, but plenty of slack is available in the organizational system of a university. In some degree, this

Element of the Normal Accident Theory	*Summary of the Element*
High-Risk Systems	Systems encompassing risks "for the operators, passengers, innocent bystanders, and for future generations," and applies to "enterprises [that] have catastrophic potential, the ability to take the lives of hundreds of people in one blow, or to shorten or cripple the lives of thousands or millions more."
Interactive Complexity	A system in which two or more discrete failures can interact in unexpected ways is described as "interactively complex." In many cases, these unexpected interactions can affect supposedly redundant sub-systems. A sufficiently complex system can be expected to have many such unanticipated failure mode interactions, making it vulnerable to normal accidents.
Tight Coupling	The sub-components of a tightly coupled system have prompt and major impacts on each other. If what happens in one part has little impact on another part, or if everything happens slowly (in particular, slowly on the scale of human thinking times), the system is not described as "tightly coupled." Tight coupling also raises the odds that operator intervention will make things worse, since the true nature of the problem may well not be understood correctly.
Incomprehensibility	A normal accident typically involves interactions that are "not only unexpected, but are incomprehensible for some critical period of time." The people involved just don't figure out quickly enough what is really going wrong. A normal accident occurs in a complex system, one that has so many parts that it is likely that something is wrong with more than one of them at any given time. A well-designed complex system will include redundancy, so that each fault by itself does not prevent proper operation. However, unexpected interactions, especially with tight coupling, may lead to system failure.

Element of the Normal Accident Theory	Summary of the Element
Operator Error	It is indeed the case that people sometimes do really stupid things, but when most of the accidents in a particular type of system (airplane, chemical plant, etc.) are blamed on the operator, that is a symptom that the operators may be confronted with an impossible task, that there is a system design problem. In a typical normal accident, the operator's actions may contribute to the problem, or even initiate the sequence of events, but the characteristics of tight coupling and interactive complexity also make their contributions.
For want of a nail . . .	The old parable about the kingdom lost because of a thrown horseshoe has its parallel in many normal accidents: the initiating event is often, taken by itself, seemingly quite trivial. Because of the system's complexity and tight coupling, however, events cascade out of control to create a catastrophic outcome.
Organizations	Organizational issues routinely confront the analyst of normal accidents. Because the interactions among subsystems are not predictable, the operators must be able to take prompt and independent action. Because of the tight coupling, in which operators of one part of the system influence the tasks confronting operators of other parts of the system, centralized control is required. These two conflicting requirements cannot be readily resolved, and the organizational attributes that work well for one side are likely to be dysfunctional for the other.

slack arises from bureaucratic replication across a university and within a college in that university.

Long time horizons also allow for university bureaucracies to rectify mistakes before they become catastrophic. Further, the extensive committee review and oversight simultaneously create organizational complexity as well as mitigate its worst effects. Certainly, plenty of mistakes occur at universities, but with abundant oversight and time to address problems, few of them ever generate consequences as obviously and immediately significant as airliners crashing or nuclear reactors melting down.

Schools and school systems—the subjects of this book—are like universities in this way; they are loosely coupled complex systems. Organizationally, a school, as a system, has slack to absorb day-to-day management issues. For example, the school will meet its daily functions even if a teacher cannot make it to work one day. The school shifts people around, doubles up some classes, gets the principal to cover, or something like this, which means the whole system continues its basic functioning without much serious consequence.

With respect to pedagogy, schools are probably both loose and linear—that is, the least given to normal accidents. Think of the replication and repetition that goes into the practice of the same skills and ideas that a student does over thirteen years of primary education. While too many missed school days can undermine or diminish a student's education, no particular day is so consequential that it can't be made up. Indeed, some hard-working students can miss weeks at a stretch and still complete the work that generates the academic growth that schooling seeks to deliver. Such situations are far from ideal, but the loose organizational system allows students the chance to correct and adjust before the "problem" becomes unmanageable.

On the other hand, schools are complex in the simultaneity and predictable divergence in the roles and goals of some of the constituent sub-systems within a school. The sports teams, the arts programs, and the math departments—to name just a few—all have different goals and perception of their and others' roles. Add in the counselors, administrators and parents, and, of course, the students, each with a dizzying variety of interests and goals, and complication, if not outright complexity, mounts dramatically.

To put it another way, numerous stakeholders (as everyone seems to enjoy calling them), each express different and sometimes divergent expectations and views about how best to meet Billy's and Susie's educational needs. Every school has its share of stories in which a student slated to participate in a reading or math support class prior to the standardized testing does not do so because the band or choir or art teacher doesn't want the student removed from his/her class (which is the only time the reading class is available), and the parents demand band over reading, against the administrator's encouraging.

While it's important that Billy "have success at band" and "enjoy school," if he doesn't meet standards on the reading and math exams, it will count as a "failure," plain and simple, for the school. But if Billy does take the support class and pass the exam, he would likely think the school failed him inasmuch as he didn't get to stay in band, the class he preferred. If Billy left band to take the reading support class and still failed the standardized reading test, it would be a kind of double failure.

This over-simplified example illustrates the way the views of student preferences and needs diverge, depending on goals and values of the person doing the viewing. (Billy's goals may not be at all like his math teacher's goals for him, for instance.) Further, this competition of goals and values is compounded in small school districts—which is the great majority of districts in the United States, where curricular and organizational options tend to be more limited by the organizational realities of staffing in small districts.

So, the education system is subject to normal accidents (if we mean "failing to meet" not just standard but a variety of other expectations beyond the testing) in that the whole system—from home and parents to the school house and classrooms—must meet the needs of an incredibly wide variety of students with variant levels of preparation, commitment, and support.

Schools experience normal accidents because of the way organizational constraints encourage and compel teachers and administrators to redefine the organizational goals as "meeting standard" in some few test areas for all students. This narrows the work of the organization by elevating a few specific goals above all the others, thereby making it too easy for school staff to miss or minimize other needs and goals that a student—or his/her parents—might have.

It's not for a lack of interest, care, or concern for a student that a teacher or administrator would hold the test scores in higher regard than a student's drama club success. The "system" demands that school staff do so, and this will only intensify as the movement to link student test scores to teacher evaluations gathers momentum.

Education and schools are obviously a bit different from the high-risk systems under consideration in the typical normal accident examples. Schools' accidents are not deadly, but they do have lasting impact. Moreover, if you spend any time in a discussion about school reform, it won't be long before someone speaks of the "high stakes" (so-called high-stakes testing is but the most obvious example), which is another way of pointing to a kind of high risk.

The consequences of failures—of and in schools—are serious, though not deadly, and long term rather than immediate. The small discrete normal accidents a student may endure throughout an educational career will only show their worst effects over time, when the cumulative result of all the accidents manifests as failure to "get an education."

Unlike an immediately catastrophic normal accident that results from quickly moving but incomprehensible failures, such as a nuclear core meltdown, each discrete normal accident of education—failed courses, failed annual tests, upward promotion without adequate academic performance—is indiscernible in its contribution to the cumulative and general failure because each makes such a small contribution to the greater accident.

Their small size makes them incomprehensible in a different kind of way. Indeed, perhaps "ignorable" is a better word. A failed course here or a failed state test there does not constitute failure to get an education, and a student can always move up to the next grade in the hope of doing better at the next level.

While the discrete failures—and finally the general catastrophic failure—are identifiable, these are the result of other failures within the whole "system" of a child's educational process. Along the way to this result, the functioning of the various parts of the education system can remain somewhat incomprehensible—or perhaps inscrutable, at least to the school and its staff. For instance, when a struggling student has weak or low levels of support at home, which can have a deleterious effect on the student's performance, the school staff often has incomplete or inaccurate understanding of those difficulties.

Since humans usually don't collapse and "fail" in such obvious and dramatic ways as airplanes when they crash, the "muddling through" that struggling students do will be retroactively understood as contributing to failure, once that failure is later identified. Students who muddle through difficulties outside of school and still do well (or at least well enough) in school never show up as "a problem."

The longer a student languishes in normal accidents, though, the more difficult it becomes to reverse the cumulative consequence of years of these small normal accidents. To the degree, then, that normal accidents of school and education only become "comprehensible" in that the likelihood of general failure is acknowledged, it may be "too late" to address those discrete problems and redeem the general "get an education" goal.

We will see shortly that this arises in part because of the fact that education deals with the complexity of developing brains rather than simply mechanically or digitally ordered machines that are designed with the intention to routinely repeat the same sets of actions. Brains, in other words, are significantly more complicated than nuclear power plants or airplanes.

Organizationally speaking, the risks, or the stakes, mount because the accidents are small and their consequences incomprehensible or ignorable. Further, much of the reform enacted in the last ten years has increased the emphasis on test results as a measure of teacher performance. This has the effect of narrowing our view—or at least assessment—of what education is and schools do, while those same reforms demand that the organizations called schools actually do increasingly more.

The awkward part of all this, especially for schools as organizational decision makers, is that plenty of students who end up getting thoroughly educated have discrete failures along the way. This is why vesting so much in any one set of measures—like annual standardized tests—distresses people in the education business. A hard-working student who succeeded in many things, just not the all-important state tests, may well have gotten educated, but would not be called such, especially as more states peg test success to graduation requirements. On the other hand, plenty of students perform very well on the tests that matter, but squander all the other non-test educational opportunities.

In other words, the varied, supple, and nuanced processes of "getting an education," and determining whether a student has done so, are vexingly difficult to measure by way of a few concrete and finite markers—like an annual standardized test—unless those markers really capture the rich breadth of the education accomplished in and for that student. In a later chapter, we will see that the current battery of standardized tests does an inadequate—if not poor—job of such measuring.

For now, this brings us to the question of what the "education system" is and who the operators are. Also, who is responsible to deal with the various manifestations of operator failure? If the system is the parents, home, community, and school, then the operator is the individual student who is receiving the wide variety of inputs into his/her education. If the system is just the schools, then the operators are the teachers and other school personnel who are delivering education to students.

If we call the schools "the system," we in effect leave indiscernible the functioning of the other parts of the student's educational life, and leave the student as something of a cipher, an entity being acted upon rather than a principal-operator of an educational system created—by his/her parents *and* the schools—to make an education available to him/her.

Think back to the Johnny who can't read. His situation arose from a cascade of events. Perhaps it was a cascade of bad or inattentive teachers. Or, a cascade of school and teachers monitoring and intervening, but other parts of the whole system (parents, student, etc.) not responding. The former happens, no doubt, but so does the latter.

In the most common form, a school identifies a student who needs an intervention in math or reading, and suggests a one-quarter class for this, but the parents opt to keep their student in band or art. The school will be held responsible if the student fails the reading test. And the school is credited nothing if that student really shines in band.

This brings us full circle to the way that schools and education are high-risk systems. The initiating event at the beginning of the cascade that ends with the normal failure of "not getting an education" will be an incredibly small event. Perhaps it was precious little time spent reading to the child, even before school started, or it was a series of teachers who let the marginally sub-par math and reading skills go by unaddressed, or maybe it was the social promotion that allowed teachers, administrators, and parents to pass a growing problem on to next year's teacher.

Educational failures have myriad sources, though, which makes discovering and implementing a collective cause and solution applicable to all, or even most, students a complex and complicated demand in itself. Indeed, the programs, interventions, or responses that result in failure for some students generate acceptable outcomes for others. To take the easiest example, while Johnny couldn't read because he was learning by whole language rather than phonics, Jimmy, Janey, and Susie learned to read just fine.

The fact of the matter is, every pedagogical approach, philosophy, or device will fail to reach at least some of the kids, and no pedagogy reaches every single student, at least not upon first delivery. If nothing else, since education is undertaken by people in relationship with each other, and the quality of that education is partly based on the quality of that relationship, some number of students in any classroom environment will get more and some less out of that relationship.

If only it were a missing nail that we needed to supply for the education kingdom to be saved. Instead, some students need a nail for their shoes, while others need a needle to sew up their haberdashery. Both pieces of metal bind material together, though by different procedures, and both are similarly shaped, but they require very different skills to use. And this farcical analogy is just the tip of the complicated iceberg.

Education as a system works best when it is loosely coupled, so the various operators—or agents—in the system have the independent capacity to address and overcome discrete failures here and there. But schools and school personnel are increasingly bound, not independent, in their actions. This goes so far as school districts telling teachers exactly what they'll be teaching on a given day. And, of course, raising the stakes on the standardized tests will incentivize teachers to focus even more on the test, and, for some, to even cheat.

In other words, the organizational environment and logic are trending toward less, not more, independent action for the teachers and school staff. Centralizing control over a situation founded on the relationships among the disparate and dispersed individuals in the system will work against those relationships and the work done through them.

The main argument advanced here is that schools—and the school system—are becoming more complex and somewhat more tightly coupled organizations. The institutional arrangements and relationships embedded in this increasingly complex organizational environment undergo a concomitant increase in complexity, and thereby suffer greater risk of normal accidents. The very regulations and programs created to make schools and students more successful also evoke—at the same time—greater risk of failures.

Undoubtedly, nobody intends these failures, and, indeed, policy makers may not even have imagined some of the failures subsequently experienced. As with any institutional arrangement, school reforms or new policy programs bind behaviors (of school staff) at the same time as they enable new, unforeseen behaviors.

The (second) Bush administration's landmark education legislation, nick-named No Child Left Behind (NCLB), exemplifies the double-edged reality of this situation. One result of the rules and requirements to show that schools were effective in providing students a good education was to stimulate the standardized testing juggernaut. What had for years been one part of the package for assessing students (the Iowa Test of Basic Skills, for instance, is nearly eighty years old) has transformed into a fundamental measure of a student's yearly performance and a school's general success in providing education.

In other words, in a kind of complexity Perrow didn't much discuss, one monitoring device gives information on two very different—and differently complicated—organizational processes. We will consider the strengths and weaknesses of standardized tests in a later chapter, so for now a general conceptual explanation of NCLB's failure will suffice.

Even assuming the best of intentions, NCLB ultimately reflects and sustains a failure of trust and civility. As the fabric of social relations has unraveled the last forty years, trust has declined and lawyering has risen. In his invaluable book, *Bowling Alone*, Robert Putnam points out that social capital (networks of richly varied relational connections among people, especially in groups) correlates with trust. High social capital, high trust, and society, including schools, "works" better.[5]

He also points out that the per capita number of lawyers in the United States was constant from 1900 to 1970. But when social capital really began to drop—in the mid-1960s—lawyering took off, because, he pithily observes, lawyers create synthetic trust. In short, low social capital, low trust, and society doesn't "work" as well. And, along the way, we come to rely more on legal authority than trust relationships.

So, law, contracts, and lawyers have increasingly become the mechanism by which problems get solved. One result is that we rely more and more on external authorities (the state paramount among them) to decide on best outcomes and mandate their pursuit. Lawyers, per se, are not the problem. Rather, as trust and social capital have declined people have turned to lawyers more and more in order to get that trust replacement. Lawyering rose as a response to the trust crisis; lawyering did not cause it.

But once set in motion, the process moves ahead inexorably. The authority of the state and laws is comprehensive and definitive, transcending any trust-built choices coming out of actual relationships among people. Why bother figuring things out, since the state just mandates anyway, and the stakeholders—parents, teachers, administrators, and so forth—find themselves tempted to jockey for political position rather than do the difficult work of relationship-building.

A teachers' strike in Tacoma, Washington, in 2011 highlighted precisely this problem. Urgent legal arguments by lawyers on both sides were only finally resolved by heading to a higher government authority—the state's governor, who told both sides to figure it out, which they then did. Indeed, one Washington newspaper said both sides were "called into the principal" to solve the dispute.[6] But all the nearly inscrutable laws and regulations mandating so much of what schools and teachers do, and the resort to state authority to enforce those mandates, makes relational trust not only more difficult to maintain, but almost anachronistic.

The "cover your backside" mentality can't help but grow stout in such an environment. Plenty of good teachers who want to do interesting and enriching work with students ultimately feel the impulse to retreat to the "just give them a worksheet" mentality in order to avoid having to justify their plans that don't fit the regulatory expectations. Or, those same teachers find themselves with less and less time available to do things outside the curriculum, as that curriculum gets mapped tighter and more comprehensively onto each of the 180 school days.

Picture all this by imagining the implications of something like an NCLB law. Presumably, without such a law, schools and teachers would leave children behind. And apparently, the best way to make sure they don't is to craft extensive regulations and dispense mandates from on high that require schools to not leave children behind. And the opportunity—or, perhaps, necessity—for people to actually work together corrodes a bit more.

The Obama administration's Race to the Top is no better. Any program that dangles federal money in front of a school district, requiring arbitrary and drastic policies, like dismissing half of a school staff as a condition of winning the money, encourages district leadership to think of the money over the relationships, and trust takes another hit.

The modern history of school reform shows this recent trend as part of a larger and longer pattern. Though he supports efforts to keep working toward the right reforms, Center for Education Policy president Jack Jennings unwittingly supports the points made here. Namely, school reforms mandated from some place beyond or outside the social and institutional environment of schools will likely miss the mark. In his own words, summarizing decades of reform efforts, Jennings says,

> Over the past fifty years, U.S. school reform has been dominated by three major movements, aimed at promoting equity, increasing school choice, and using academic standards to leverage improvement. While all three have changed schooling in notable ways, none has brought about the needed level of

general improvements because they mostly sought to improve education from the outside rather than the inside. [7]

The first and third trend—promoting equity and using standards—continue to affect school processes and functioning today. Without delving more deeply than necessary at this point, the underlying emphasis of the equity-promoting reforms has been to ensure equal access to education for previously marginalized or disadvantaged groups. The process started with racial minorities, and worked its way from there to include gender equity, socio-economic equity, and equity for children with special educational needs. Obviously, each of these requirements remains in place, each new category having been added to those already covered.

The standards movement began—slowly—in the first Bush administration and continued under Clinton, but really took off in the second Bush administration. Again, Jack Jennings:

> The enactment of NCLB in 2002 was a turning point for the standards movement. Instead of academic standards serving as a focal point to raise the quality of instruction in schools, test-driven accountability became the norm. Teachers understood that if their students did not pass the annual state accountability tests, their schools would be labeled as "failing" by the news media because of the penalties prescribed by NCLB. [8]

Jennings goes on to point out that the standards movement has generated clearer expectations of what students should be learning in school, which, in theory, is a good thing. But, combine this clarity with what might fairly be called teachers' "accountability anxiety," and teaching to the test—at least in some degree—becomes a rational choice for teachers. And to the extent that such test emphasis arises, what students should learn in school more and more becomes all (or, at least more) of what they do learn in school.

(Increasing school choice—the second of the three reform trends—is something more of an argument about alternative structures and arrangements than changing existing school functions. Vouchers come the closest to creating a mechanism that incentivizes schools to distinguish themselves in a competitive environment, but even here the real intent of vouchers is to give individuals—students and their families—the opportunity to choose their own school, not change the nature of existing schools. Individual school leaders may decide to transform their schools, but this is not mandated, as with equity and standards. A later chapter will address vouchers and charters.)

To this point we have reviewed the ways that organizational complexity has been growing in schools and the school system. The brain is also a complex system, subject to similar concerns regarding what is probably better called normal variance, rather than accidents. Increasingly complex school systems are working with amazingly complex and widely varying brains. If Perrow's logic regarding complexity and normal accidents has any analytical force, we must face the implications of an increasingly complex system addressing the needs of another complex system.

Though this is not Perrow's specific argument, it is a little enough stretch to think that raising the complexity of the system that works with and for another complex system raises the overall complexity all the more. For one thing, we had better get the new regulatory and monitoring processes right, or else we increase the prospects that the normal variances in complex brains will become even harder to identify and address with the increasingly complicated system of education, because the bureaucratic complexity will tend toward rigidity, not flexibility.

An example from another realm illustrates the problem. Complicated technology doing the complex job of maintaining security against invasive threats raises its own set of issues, specifically that the fail points in technology are not discovered and addressed by the technology's creators, which leaves a fatal weak spot in the complicated technology.

Shortly after the September 11 terror attacks in 2001, Charles Mann[9] wrote at length about why we should be careful—perhaps even skeptical—about relying on sophisticated (and complex) technologies to recognize and protect against security threats. Mann detailed the surprisingly simple ways to foil security technologies. He points out, for instance, that many fingerprint readers can be tricked by simply breathing on the monitor's sensor, thereby bringing back the last fingerprint observed. Others could be beaten with some graphite powder and adhesive tape. Face recognition software is beatable with high-resolution photographs of approved faces with pupil holes cut out so that real pupils will be registered by the technology.[10]

While people cannot walk through airports with paper photographs of approved faces, face recognition software is notoriously problematic anyway. Even if such software were effective high into the ninety-ninth percentile, it would register hundreds of false positives each day in each of the largest U.S. airports. As Mann observes, such performance would compel us to ignore this complicated technology.

Indeed, Mann notes that though not all the technologies (at that time) perform as poorly as this, "all of them fail badly."[11] Recent revelations about hackers taking over the computer controls of two popular automobiles,[12] or interrupting insulin pumps,[13] demonstrates how complex technologies still have weak spots that make them vulnerable to catastrophic intrusion.

The point is that complex systems dealing with complex situations or circumstances generate failure, and probably do so at an even higher rate than one complex system on its own. Mann cites security expert Bruce Schneier to support his observation that low-technology systems—like human observation—are still a necessary part of effective security systems.

Nobody takes airline security more seriously than the Israelis, and intensive low-tech human systems remain an essential part of their work to protect air transport into and out of their country. All that to say, complex systems dealing with complex situations (or other complex systems) amounts to at least as much—and probably more—overall difficulty as one complex system alone.

Education is an increasingly complex "system," and the brain has always been an astoundingly complicated organ. John Medina puts it simply in "Brain Rule #3: Every brain is wired differently."[14] The physiological complexity alone boggles the mind, so to speak. As Bronson and Merryman point out, every cubic millimeter of an adult brain contains an estimated 35 to 70 million neurons and as many as 500 billion synapses.[15]

The nerve fibers in that same cubic millimeter would cover twenty miles, if laid end to end. This neural density is what drove the thinking that a thicker cortex (i.e., more gray matter) correlated with higher intelligence. Recent findings show, however, that the very smartest children actually have thinner cortices, until later in their childhood. The supersmart added cortical thickness for years after their peers had stopped. They developed their exceptional intelligence later than typical, in other words.

It is not clear why, yet, but intellectual activities can be housed in a variety of places in different brains, and this can affect intellectual performance. Your critical language area (CLA) is what makes you competent with the language you are reading right now. And if your CLA is housed in the superior temporal gyrus area, you will not be as effective with language as people whose brains host the CLA elsewhere. Further, the smaller or tighter the neural footprint of your CLA, the better you'll do with language.[16]

Brains also "upgrade" at different times and rates, and may do so based on what use each brain is put to. Neurons that get more use add a layer of white fatty insulation, which makes those neurons more efficient. The brain region associated with verbal knowledge growth—the left hemisphere—picks up speed in middle childhood, while the area associated with high-level reasoning matures last, in preadolescence. Of course, if a brain is not compelled to engage much verbal material—and instead plays video games more—those neurons will compete with other neurons to develop the higher efficiency upgrading.

Another complexity of the learning process derives from the fact that the brain moves the locations of its cognitive functioning. Brain scans show up to forty different locations (or neural clusters) operating while performing even simple verbal tasks, but many of those locations have moved from youth to adulthood. How well the brain learns to make these shifts greatly affects "a child's ultimate intellectual success."

All of this undermines the idea that we can or should try to identify so-called highly capable children any earlier than middle school. Yet such programs are increasingly touted as the best route to academic success, at least for the schools as a system. The Washington state legislature, for instance, recently mandated that every school district must have a K-12 highly capable program by 2014.

Clearly, legislatures and policy makers see highly capable programs as the institutional design through which supposedly greater college readiness will be made available or created. The mere presence of the program does little if it's badly managed, though. And most are badly managed. Most pressing is that of one hundred kids identified as gifted—that is, the smartest—in kindergarten, only twenty-seven of those continue to qualify in third grade.[17] Unless we are content to exclude later-blooming highly capable kids, such programs must reassess students later, and adjust the enrollment in the program. Bronson and Merryman point out that few, if any schools, do so.

To put it mildly, brain development is dauntingly complex. Addressing the varying educational needs possessed by complex brains in different statuses of capacity and readiness is daunting, and made more difficult when done by a complex—rather than simpler—educational system. Apparently, education reform is predicated on the notion that the growing organizational complexity of schools would better deal with the varying and diverse needs of different and complex brains. The increasing programmatic complexity reflects greater richness in production and delivery of education, a richness intended to serve more students better.

It's a double-edged sword, though. The greater breadth intended to enrich learning for students with wider sets of needs also serves to increase the complexity of the education system and of schools, and thereby increases the likelihood of normal accidents at the same time. At the risk of oversimplifying, when we create increasingly complex organizational systems to deal with complex organisms called students, we expand service for some students while also foreordaining a greater number of normal accidents in the system.

The standardized test process abets this reality. Causing a narrow emphasis on what constitutes success, and measuring each student by that, and expecting that each and every student can meet that standard simply by dint of age (rather than more nuanced markers of development) so fundamentally shrinks the field of view as to leave much of the complex educational process largely out of focus.

Ultimately, shrinking or blurring the picture in this way jeopardizes effective operation of the education system, no matter whom we identify as the operators. Dick Piccard provides the best explanation of this:

> System operators [students, parents, teachers, etc., but not reformers and policy makers] must make decisions, even with ambiguous information. The pro-

cess of making a tentative choice also creates a mental model of the situation. When following through on the initial choice, the visible results are compared to those expected on the basis of that initial mental model. Provided that the first few steps' results are consistent, the fact that the mental model was tentative is likely to be forgotten, even if later results contradict it. They become "mysterious" or "incomprehensible" rather than functioning as clues to the falsity of the earlier tentative choice. This is simply the way the human mind works, and systems designed with contrary expectations of their operators are especially vulnerable to system accidents.[18]

Everybody—parents, teachers, and even reformers—makes educational decisions based on incomplete information, and they each do so with a different target population in mind. Parents are concerned about their children, teachers about all their students, and reformers about the whole system. The decisions each one makes, then, must vie with the decisions the other groups would like to make, each relying on their particular view of the educational forest.

Each group also develops its own mental models of what ought to be done, and how to accomplish that. The differing perceptions and expectations arising from these models can easily create divergence, if not contradiction, of preferences and plans, thereby stimulating concerns—in each group—that the system is operating contrary to appropriate norms and expectations. In short, a special kind of inter-group incomprehensibility follows from this particular organizational complexity. More programs, more regulations, more thorough assessments (of teachers or students) will not ameliorate the problems derived from this complexity . . . they will make it worse.

In this chapter, we saw how enlarging organizational structures and increasing regulatory demands make schools both more complex and tightly bound institutions, and thereby raise the prospect of normal failures of the education system and its component elements—schools and students. Brains are also incredibly complex, making the educational task varied and complicated without the added organizational complexity. Next, we consider the ways that the climate of expectations adds to the pressure on schools and staff.

NOTES

1. Charles Perrow, *Normal Accidents: Living with High-Risk Technologies* (New York: Basic Books, 1984).

2. Diane Vaughan, *The Challenger Launch Decision: Risky Technology, Culture, and Deviance at NASA*, (Chicago: University of Chicago Press, 1996).

3. William Langewiesche, "The Lessons of Valujet 592." *The Atlantic*, March 1, 1998. http://www.theatlantic.com/magazine/archive/1998/03/the-lessons-of-valujet-592/306534/.

4. Dick Piccard, Ohio University, "Book Review: *Normal Accidents*." Last modified April 14, 2011. http://www.ohio.edu/people/piccard/entropy/perrow.html.

5. Robert Putnam, *Bowling Alone: The Collapse and Revival of American Community* (New York: Simon & Schuster, 2001).

6. Jim Camden and Jonathan Brunt, "Tacoma Schools, teachers being called to Principal Gregoire's office," *The Spokesman-Review*, September 21, 2011. http://www.spokesman.com/blogs/spincontrol/2011/sep/21/tacoma-schools-teachers-being-called-principal-gregoires-office/.

7. Jack Jennings, *Why Have We Fallen Short and Where Do We Go From Here?*(Manuscript, Center on Education Policy, 2012), p. 12.

8. Ibid., p. 5.

9. Charles Mann, "Homeland Insecurity," *The Atlantic*, September 2002. http://www.theatlantic.com/magazine/archive/2002/09/homeland-insecurity/302575/.

10. See also, Patrick O'Neil, "Complexity and Counterterrorism: Thinking About Biometrics," *Studies in Conflict & Terrorism*, 28, no. 6 (2005): 547-566, http://www.tandfonline.com/doi/abs/10.1080/10576100591008962.

11. Mann, "Homeland Insecurity."

12. Douglas Newcomb, "Hackers take over a Prius, call for automakers to patch security holes," *MSN Autos* (blog), July 29, 2013, http://editorial.autos.msn.com/blogs/post--hackers-take-over-a-prius-call-for-automakers-to-patch-security-holes.

13. Kim Carollo, "Can Your Insulin Pump Be Hacked?" *ABC News: Medical Unit* (blog), April 10, 2012, http://abcnews.go.com/blogs/health/2012/04/10/can-your-insulin-pump-be-hacked/.

14. John Medina, *Brain Rules: 12 Principles for Surviving and Thriving at Work, Home, and School* (Seattle: Pear Press, 2008), chap. 3.

15. Po Bronson and Ashley Merryman, *NurtureShock: New Thinking About Children* (New York: Twelve, 2009), 110-112.

16. Medina, *Brain Rules,* p. 66.

17. Ibid., 97.

18. Piccard, "Book Review: *Normal Accidents.*"

Chapter Three

Complexity and the Social Conversation

In the previous chapters we saw how schools and the school system operate in an environment of organizational complexity, addressing complex and varied brains. In this chapter, we add the complicated social discussion about schools and education to discern the particular—and perhaps peculiar—construction of the issues, questions, and answers to "the problem" with schools. The complication arising from these convoluted conversations results in heightened, but confusing or divergent, expectations in an already organizationally complex environment, thereby raising the likelihood of normal accidents even higher.

The social conversation about education and schools is confused and confusing. Most people experience schools locally and individually, but the elite discussants tend to focus their conversation on the system, in a general and, what we'll call here, national way, though individual schools or even classrooms serve as demonstration or evidence in the discussion.

The natural impulse to generalize from particular experience up to the supposed wider pattern leaves the uninitiated (parents, and other education "outsiders") flummoxed by the aloofness following from the insiders' conversation, and the insiders (school staff and education reformers—though the two have different perspectives) despairing that the outsiders "just don't understand."

At root, language and terms contribute to a significant amount of the vexation. Parents don't want to talk about "best practices," "power standards," or "data teaming." They just want to know their child is doing well in a good school. And while parents have been increasingly trained to see their child's performance as indicated by the results on the standardized test, they see even this marker differently than school staff. Educators, after all, operationalize this measure of their general performance in terms of aggregate, not individual, outcomes on the test. So parents and staff are looking at the same indicator, but with very different purposes.

To move that aggregate result in the desired direction, school staff do indeed implement best practice approaches that take account of information gathered from data teaming. Parents, by contrast, just want to know how their child will do better on the test. Thus begins the most fundamental divergence in perception and understanding in the social discussion about education and schools.

Every profession and avocation maintains its own specialized and technical language. To those outside the select group, this seems off-putting, perhaps even designed to marginalize those outsiders, thereby allowing insiders to speak above the heads of outsiders and effectively build a protective hedge around those inside.

At the risk of overgeneralizing, this exclusionary process is probably getting worse in education, in tandem with the increasing "technical complexity" inhering in the specialized language. Whether using specialized words, or, more typically, common words with specialized meanings, explaining things like the Common Core State Standards, power standards, test strands, high-yield strategies, the taxonomy of learning, or the difference between an EALR and a GLE, a CBA and a CBPA, and the old state test and the new one, not to mention the dizzying array of government programs, can overwhelm even education insiders, let alone parents and other outsiders.

This disconnect between insiders (educators and reformers) and outsiders (parents and others) adds confusion to the complexity and magnifies the skewing of the conversation—the outsiders focus more emphatically on their particular experience of their own schools, while the insiders retrench to their specialized knowledge and understanding. In other words, the language more likely deepens the disconnects and intensifies when the complexity and the confusion mount.

Overlaid on the insider-outsider dynamic is something of a national-local dichotomy. Education groups, reformers, activists, and experts engage in a discussion of schools writ large, or of education, as socially ordered by our philosophically constructed views and values.

These discussions or debates are imbalanced, though. Most parents are local outsiders, whereas most experts are something more like national insiders, participating in the broader discussion as insiders using generalizations that are too often narrowly gathered—either in local conditions or according to specific and finite measures. The desires, needs, and experiences of the two groups differ, no doubt, but both local groups—parents and school staff—are granted little role in the discussions of schools. Since much of the analysis, critique, and debate focuses on teachers, so it is here.

Educators and staff are governed and "trained" by experts whose expertise can often seem—at least to those they're training—theoretically and practically removed from real classroom life. At the same time, teachers, administrators, and staff are the primary access point for parents to engage in the wider discussion of what schools are and should be. Local education professionals, then, are thought too inexpert to engage in the wider debate about education, but they are the front line of serving students and parents, the primary subjects of the programs these same local professionals are unworthy to participate in discussing.

This situation creates its own variant of complexity and complication, contributing to the likelihood of normal failure. The national discussion generates programs, procedures, and expectations for local—and disconnected—educators to implement. When those directives seem at odds with local experience, educators struggle to reconcile the difference. Some wholeheartedly embrace the directives, protected by the "we were told to" hedge. Others simply ignore the directives, navigating the school organizational hierarchy accordingly. And still others try to adapt or mold the directives to the local circumstances.

Each response has different consequences for teaching and learning. The latter two responses leave much in the individual teachers' hands, while the first response cedes pedagogical authority to decision makers higher up the food chain. Following one of the latter two paths requires more social and organizational effort and resources for each individual teacher, but to take either of these paths also raises risks . . . for the individual teacher and for the "system," as such divergences, again, generate a kind of incoherence in the structure of that school.

In other words, if individual staff members respond differently, the school qua organization increases in another kind of complexity. This, then, is the general tenor of the social discussion about schools and education, especially as seen and experienced by teachers.

To see how strident the conversation can turn, consider an outsider who went national. In 2011, Amy Chua—a law professor—created a minor storm with her book *Battle Hymn of the Tiger Mother*.[1] Chua, who was arguing about parenting style as much as education, detailed the benefits of hard-nosed parenting, especially when compared to the coddling she claims most American parents are doing now.

The book stirred up quite a bit of controversy (which helped stir up sales, no doubt). Chua appeared on or made statements that were picked up by national news outlets across the media spectrum, from *The Wall Street Journal*[2] to National Public Radio.[3] And the issue still burns brightly; in spring 2013, Kim Wong Kelter released *Tiger Babies Strike Back*,[4] a memoir critiquing the parenting that Chua extols.

The point here is that much of that discussion casts parenting as a choice between high expectations and nurturing, or, more precisely, the proper balance between the two—that is to say, whether parents push their children, even sometimes demandingly, or they support and encourage their children's gifts as expressed by their individual personalities.

Teachers can feel themselves caught between the two poles, as well. Writing less stridently than Chua, Amanda Sheaffer expresses her concern that the demands of test preparation inhibit real nurturing, which her "gut" tells her is better. She describes feeling torn, saying, as if speaking to her students, "I am caught in a struggle between what I have been told to do and what you deserve."[5]

Sheaffer's anxiety reflects one of the timeless dilemmas teachers feel about their own intuition regarding craft practice, but more to the point, such dichotomization overdraws and overdramatizes the situation. It seems unclear that tests and nurturing must be mutually exclusive. No doubt, they overlap at least some.

To say that the tests and nurturing are mutually exclusive is to say that the testing process actually captures or evaluates nothing of what real nurturing teaching produces. Good teaching should—and will, in fact—both nurture and produce at least some learning outcomes that will be captured on the test.

Ideally, the test should capture evidence that teachers have done a good job nurturing a child. Nurture well and widely, create good outcomes, and the test becomes something of an afterthought. One may easily demonstrate that the current tests do not accomplish this ideal very well, but that does not prove it impossible that the test could capture a decent portion of the "right" (i.e., nurturing) stuff.

Framing the debate according to this dichotomy, though, is largely instrumental—what's the best balance for maximization of your child? And in so rendering it, we make a monolith of both nurture and test outcomes. In other words, the discussion is constructed in dichotomous terms that compel us to embrace one or the other extreme. Support nurture against the test, as if in so doing you can create just what every child precisely needs. Choose the test, by contrast, and you'll demonstrate that you've taught every child everything he/she needs to know.

Further, constructing the discussion this way lacks thoughtfulness about the content of those expectations—what, exactly, should we maximize on? The answer to this is clear for Chua, who famously (or infamously) insisted her daughters play violin or piano only. "Playing the drums," she says, "leads to drugs."[6]

Interestingly, the significance of parental involvement underlies both lines of reasoning. They argue over the best way parents can make their children all that they can be. But half of all children, like half of all adults, are, by definition, below average (Lake Wobegon notwithstanding). For instance, no amount of practice—even the Gladwellian 10,000 hours—could make many of us anything more than practiced hacks at ballet or golf or singing.

It is unreasonable for us to assume that everyone can achieve the same transcendent heights in whatever particular activity or discipline one chooses, just by working hard enough. Indeed, the move toward standards and standardized testing tacitly admits this. Schools and teachers are being assessed on how well their students meet these generalized basic expectations, not on how high the best students fly while at their school.

Standardization's appeal rests on the fact that we should be able to expect that everyone can learn a basic minimum set of skills and material. This seemingly more reasonable expectation entered the discussion—initially at the national level, by way of an academic, then eventually to the local outsider level—as the "every child can learn" mantra. Unfortunately, this, too, has skewed our sense of what schools should and can do.

The rather overgeneralized claim—stated as fact—has become so bland that it shows up routinely in school board campaigns. Whether candidates invoke it as a reason to support their candidacy, or constituents question whether candidates believe it, the idea subtly shifts greater responsibility on to schools. Since every child can learn, the thinking goes, we need only find the ways that will make this happen. And if children aren't learning, then the schools must be doing something wrong. Rather clear and straightforward. The devil, of course, is in the details.

At least some scholars recognize the practical difficulty of such claims. Writing nearly twenty-five years ago—shortly after the "every child can learn" nostrum gained currency, Ronald Slavin, for instance, in his voluminous scholarship, outlined the myriad different ways that schools can support students' academic achievement, and indirectly showed that some sort of easily replicable model will not meet every child's need everywhere at all times.[7]

Slavin's observations remain true today because the overreaching—and now too boiled down—claim cannot stand in the face of logic and evidence. We can't, at the same time, speak of the variety of different learning styles, the learning consequences of different brain architectures, or the effects of variations in students' emotional circumstances, and claim there is one pedagogical model, style, or system that is going to meet the needs of thirty students with different and divergent mixes of these, and other, factors.

Moreover, it should be obvious that not all students learn at the same pace or to the same depth. This shows up particularly clearly as students advance through school. It may be reasonable (though it may not, also) to say that all five- or six-year-olds should be able to name their letters and accompanying sounds (phonemes, if you want the insider language; the smallest contrastive unit in the sound system of a language, if you want to get really technical).

As students get older, and native abilities begin to show their differences, the best practice for addressing sixth-grade Johnny's reading difficulties will be nothing like the best practice for launching Johnny's high-achieving classmate, Jonathan, to greater (Tiger Child?) heights of achievement.

Further, as students get older, whether they can learn gets complicated by what they should learn. A reader who is effective at decoding words may be able to read—accomplish the phonemic mechanics—a lot of words without having any idea what those words mean.

So, at what grade can/should a student know what *perfervid, obloquy*, and *concatenation* mean? Does every student need to know the quadratic formula? Would resources spent working on either these words or this formula possibly be better spent on something for which the student would get more educational "payoff"? What kind of rules and procedures do we need to create in order to allow such power of choice for parents and their students?

The degree to which our social conversation is rife with clichés ("what works," "best practices," etc.) and hollow rhetoric ("tougher standards," "greater student engagement," etc.), we avoid such questions, and we fundamentally miss the serious and complicated nature of what school and education are. Further, this disjuncture between our collective circumlocution and the complex reality may also have important implications for the issue of standardized testing. We will discuss the standardized test process at greater length later, so for now this summary point suffices.

Every state's standardized test has a target score called "meeting standard" (in Washington state that number is 400). Unless we set the standard (what it takes to earn 400) ludicrously low, some students will not meet it. To put it another way, a bar set so low that everybody passes doesn't really measure anything worth knowing.

The test isn't really about measuring a student's progress for his or her sake (or information or guidance). We collect the aggregate pass/fail results as a way to evaluate a school. It is, of course, an incredibly narrow measure, even on its own terms. For if we really cared about progress we'd establish a metric of growth that would register success by increases, especially for students on the lower end of the performance spectrum. But, more on that later.

We turn now, instead, to another phase of the social discussion about schools—namely, the kinds of different groups seeking to answer all these philosophical and practical questions, or at least present an understanding of schools and education that implies answers to these questions. By working our way from the national level down to the local—indeed, the family, we will see how the national-local dichotomy leaves the outsiders outside and the local insiders (school staff) frustrated.

Politics being what it is, and education—socially speaking—being incredibly political, to make a real impact on what schools are and do, one must go national. Parent groups (outsiders) who want to get on the inside understand this. Look how Parents Across America (PAA) explains who they are, in their own words:

> [PAA] is a grassroots organization that connects parents and activists from across the U.S. to share ideas and work together on improving our nation's public schools. It was founded by a group of activist parents who recognized the need to collaborate for positive change, rather than remain solely entrenched in separate battles in our local communities. Since the top-down forces that are imposing their will on our schools have become national in scope, we need to be as well. [8]

PAA is so grassroots that you cannot contact them from their web site, save to donate or sign up to receive their newsletter. In other words, you can give money (upward) by clicking on the Donate button (auto-filled with $25 as your donation), or receive their information (downward). [9] You can join them in celebrating their reception into the national educational elite status, bestowed upon them when education scholar John Owen asked PAA to write a blurb for the dust jacket of his latest book. [10] It leaves one wondering if collaboration for positive change involves more top-down leadership . . . just from a different top.

As for the organization's practical solutions, the web site continues, "We advocate for proven, progressive measures such as reducing class size and increasing parent involvement, and oppose corporate-style efforts to privatize our schools." All rather predictable, generic, and supposedly achievable with more money.

The National Parent Teacher Association indulges its own brand of similarly grandiose, but ultimately empty, rhetoric. Their motto, prominent on the web page, is "Every child, one voice." [11] High minded, but organizationally impossible, even in one classroom of thirty students, let alone across the country.

Clearly, some parent groups are more grassroots and more participatory. Start School Later is a national parents group advocating for later start times for high schools. The organization's web site [12] allows a much wider range of contact and engagement with the organization, local chapters, and other interested parents. The difference with this group lies in the narrow focus. They pursue one specific policy objective—to change school start times. Grassroots can more easily grow from one (or few) issues. Activating around a broad and extensive agenda of issues ultimately generates organizational hierarchy and leadership, and a certain amount of top-down structure.

These are but a few examples of outsider parent groups "going national." This is not intended as a comprehensive review of all the national groups. To get a comprehensive sense of how this works, though, consider Patrick McGuinn's explanation of the education reform groups' playbook:

There is both a public and private dimension to ERAO (Education Reform Advocacy Organization) work. Behind the scenes the groups work to cultivate relationships and build credibility with governors and state legislators and their professional staff as well as with state education-agency folks. They hold regular briefings for these insiders—often bringing in nationally recognized experts—to make the case for reform and report on how other states have tackled similar challenges. They also wage a very public campaign for the hearts and minds of average citizens by organizing town hall meetings with parents and publishing op-eds in state and local media. [13]

The point here is that the best way to get in the education reform game is to move up the bureaucratic hierarchy—that's where the discussion happens. Later, we will see that even local conversations involve debate about ideas and issues brought downward to the local level—the grassroots responding to issues and ideas brought from above.

Where parent groups rely on organizing, other education activist groups rely on supposedly specialized knowledge. Standardized tests, and the data they produce, enable some groups to participate in the national discussion by casting the broader social conversation about education in what looks like technical terms. With a test constructed around several academic strands whose content is more than a little inscrutable, at least to all but the most devoted insiders, and a score rendered in terms meaningless outside the context of the test itself, it takes specialized knowledge to understand how to decode the test, the results, and the teaching response to both.

This elevating of the technical further distances outsiders/parents, and opens the door for a new kind of educational expert—to wit, Bill Gates and his educational foundation. Gates's work, while technologically powerful, puts the normal accident "want of a nail" problem into new perspective. The prevalence and insistence of his (or, his foundation's) claims about the solutions to the education problem reflect more the classic "hammer in search of a nail."

Indeed there are, abroad in the culture, a great many hammers searching for nails to pound. Everyone seems to have an answer—usually presented as *the* answer—to the question of how to fix schools. Bill Gates and his foundation found the answer—ostensibly—in teachers. They took a survey of teachers to find out "what works."

The results from 40,000 teachers can't be wrong, so let's take a look at America's Teachers on America's Schools. [14] The study's conclusions are unsurprisingly compatible with the agenda the foundation has long been pursuing. The study summary offers several recommendations, all rather predictable in their generality, and typical in their rhetoric, to create better classrooms.

Innovate to reach today's students. It doesn't take a degree in computer science to guess that the study finds teachers want more digital tools because "students don't learn the way they did 10 years ago." What they really mean is that students don't use the same modalities of learning. It seems clear enough that reading, writing, and doing work (like math problems, science experiments, film-making, performance, etc.) are still the way students learn. So students make YouTube videos now instead of films.

But what are the possibilities for innovating that are not connected to, or a function of, technology? Creativity in changing school schedules, length and number of school days, or the design and scope of the standardized test arrangements (all issues we will discuss in the final chapter) could have significant impacts on student learning because they take account of the fact that, in some ways, students have learned in exactly the same ways for a long time.

Unfortunately, some of the current organizational and institutional arrangements do not match up well with those old patterns, and we should, therefore, consider reforming those outmoded institutional arrangements. To name just one, teenagers' circadian rhythms shift in such a way that starting the high school day much later in the morning would generate better student performance.[15] Regrettably, institutional inertia and competing needs of other people and groups in the situation make this particular best practice well-nigh impossible.

Establish clearer and tougher academic standards. Who doesn't plump for this? This is the equivalent of a politician saying she's for families, or he's going to create jobs. One concern in this case, though, is to make sure those innovative ways of reaching students don't slide into "easier ways" for a student to complete their school responsibilities. "Clearer" also raises its own set of concerns.

Clearer probably would require shorter, as in briefer to explain, or fewer . . . in other words, less complicated. But in the push to set standards for every academic pursuit, we have gotten more and longer standards, instead. For instance, look to see if your state has something like Classroom Based Performance Assessments for Dance or Theater or Art.[16]

Bridge school and home to raise student achievement. The survey data says that teachers think lack of support at home contributes mightily to students' struggles. It shouldn't take a survey to "confirm" what we know from life and intuition. The question really is, how do we better connect parents to schools?

The parents that really need to be "connected" are often the ones who are indifferent. Is there a way to make them more interested? A way to hold them accountable? Or, can the school simply create benefits and consequences for the student him/herself, and expect the parents to just accept this? In other words, what do we do when a parent just won't "connect"?

In a highly institutionalized and bureaucratized environment (which the next chapter will examine in greater depth), decision makers and leaders hope that more and thicker institutional arrangements will make greater connection happen. In 2013, Senator Jack Reed, (Dem., RI) sponsored legislation to set aside 0.3 percent of Title I (federal funding intended to address the educational needs of low-income students) administrative funds to support what reports have called the necessary infrastructure—institutions—to get parents involved in their schools. Says Senator Reed, "When parents are involved with their children's education it not only improves schools but also strengthens communities."[17]

Setting aside money to create something called statewide family engagement centers creates political momentum and enthusiasm, but it takes a Field of Dreams–like faith to assume that "if you build it, they will come." Institutions externally rather than organically created might make a place for relationships to happen, but it takes people willing to work at those relationships in order to create effective and durable connections.

Finally, the Gates Foundation's heartwarming clincher: *All lives have equal value.* While this reflects something of Gates's worthwhile humanitarian concerns, if Louis Menand is right, our schools do not really embody this principle. In a society as individualist as ours, the schools help students do everything they can to maximize their college potential, so they can do everything possible to maximize job prospects.

Menand observes that the education system a society gets is a function of what that society wants the system to say about what the society is like. He goes on to claim that "Americans have an egalitarian approach to inequality: they want everyone to have an equal chance to become better-off than everyone else. By and large, for most people school is the mechanism for achieving this."[18] In other words, we don't really expect schools to make everyone fantastically capable. We want schools to provide the route by which someone might become fantastically capable, if he/she works at it. Through the schools, we provide the opportunity. If you don't seize that opportunity, it's on you.

Bill Gates is only the most prominent and therefore among the most frustrating—for a lot of teachers and staff (excluded local insiders)—national figures to assert their views and values in the national debate about schools and education. If nothing else, Gates vexes because his observations and claims run so counter to his own educational upbringing. In *Outliers*, Malcolm Gladwell fawns (a bit) over Gates as an example of what one can accomplish when you get the magical 10,000 hours of practice at something—in Gates's case, computer programming.[19]

Gladwell's thesis is that time and place circumstances—to get the necessary 10,000 hours of practice—have made opportunity for the phenomenal success stories like Gates's. Gladwell rather weakly argues that we'd be better off as a society if more people got the kinds of opportunities to develop virtuosity in something, as Gates did.

The interesting part, especially when you consider Gates's somewhat simplistic solutions (get the best 25 percent of teachers to take on four or five more students, so all students can be in front of a great teacher, [20] for instance), is that, by Gladwell's reckoning, Gates's mother had an enormous impact on his development. His and several other mothers at his high school got together to help their sons start a computer club—one of the first of its kind in the country—and then helped connect that club to various important Seattle players in the nascent computer world. These activities (add-ons to his school life) got Gates a jump start in computers.

In short, Gladwell tells a story more of auto-didacticism than teacher-governed learning. This is not to say that there weren't important teachers in Gates's life, but he's not exactly the poster child for the teacher-driven success his foundation now touts. Indeed, if there is an object lesson to take, it is not that everyone needs a great teacher. Rather, from Gates we learn that if you want a better shot at success, get a mother like Mrs. Gates. Of course, along the way, you will probably also need the kind of social connections and the economic wherewithal the Gates family had. Not exactly the easiest policy options to implement, even with a dense network of family engagement centers.

So, what exactly is it that makes Bill Gates so well qualified to push these rather facile recommendations into the national discussion of education? His enormous success, of course. Trouble is, solving computer problems, or creating new solutions (in search of a problem that needs solving) with computers isn't much like teaching children. It would be great if those youngsters were coded as series of binary numbers. Alas, they are not.

While schools have some problems (and some successes), we need to ask a lot better questions in order to get better answers about where to go from here. Several things come to mind. One is, what if the questions were put differently? How many schools are failing? (What is failing, by the way?) In what ways are they failing? Or, what if we reframe the whole discussion? How about, in what ways are the schools a barometer of social failings more generally? Are the schools simply one set of the generally failing institutions in society? Or, another reframe: In what ways are the schools succeeding? What can we reasonably expect of schools?

These are more than rhetorical questions, yet they go largely unasked. Their answers, instead, are implied in other choices and programs. More importantly, teachers and school staff answer them every day with their actions. This answering may be only semi-conscious, but the patterns derived of the answers get embedded in the organizational and institutional arrangements of what schools are and do.

In this way, another layer of complexity gets added to the story. For school staff make local choices that are supposed to accommodate and account to national expectations and demands. Individual teachers typically find themselves making these daily choices, while a larger and broader social conversation continually beats on around them.

This social conversation continues on at several levels. Perhaps more precisely, several conversations go on simultaneously. We continue, then, our tour of these different conversations about education by looking briefly at the way national political actors speak.

"Clearly, the status quo isn't working for children." So claimed Arne Duncan, President Obama's Education Secretary, in a speech to a teacher's union conference in 2011. In so speaking, Duncan angered part of the traditional Democratic base—teachers—by making common cause with what had been his, and their, ideological antagonists, Republican governors.

Even more important than the politics, though, are the questions such a comment raises. Specifically, just what is the status quo? Which status are we talking about? For whom isn't it working? The "reality" of schools varies dramatically from district to district, even building to building. So talking of a national status quo simplifies the situation more than is good or helpful.

Perhaps when national political actors go local we can more clearly discern their plan to change the status quo that isn't working. Around the same time as Secretary Duncan's speech, President Obama visited a Miami school (Miami Central Senior High School) that had turned everything around, following significant parts of the president's so-called turnaround plan.[21]

Federal stimulus money helped, but "school officials said all problems can't be solved with money." Seeming to understand that people are more important than money, the school's principal assures that reforming the status quo involves "identify[ing] individuals who want to be part of the change—whether it's students, teachers or administrators—and have people here who want to be here, for the good of the cause."

This is inspiring rhetoric, and seemingly cognizant of the relational aspect of the problem, but rhetoric that generates as many questions as it answers. Do all parties agree on the cause? Are those who disagree compelled to agree, or to leave? How do we create inclusiveness in such an environment? How do you identify the students who want to be part of the change, and what do you do with the ones who don't?

At the furthest extreme, in focusing on those students and teachers who "want to be [t]here, for the good of the cause," you would be able to create a non-random group of staff and students with what sounds like higher commitment. Of course, the low-commitment students would need to go to school somewhere, too. Teachers often lament that if only those less committed students were more committed. . . . Well, this "selection" process just might solve that problem.

Further, the whole story is presented as a success of the federal deus ex machina that fixes faculties (by replacement) and thereby schools. How else are we to think about Miami-Dade Assistant Superintendent Nikolai Vitti saying, "We've replaced over 50 percent of the faculty in the last two years. . . . It's brought new energy and a greater willingness to go above and beyond for our kids." *New energy, Go above and beyond:* these are inspiring, but ultimately rather empty phrases that neither clarify nor edify.

When the president shows up to celebrate the success, though, it makes for a dramatic and newsworthy story. But we need to look closely at the numbers, as devotees of data insist. It turns out that Miami Central's turnaround has been a lot less dramatic than proclaimed when President Obama visited in the spring of 2011.

The Florida school accountability grade (itself determined by what appears to be an astoundingly complicated formula involving something called the high school acceleration rate, test score growth, at-risk student performance, weightings of all these factors, resultant supplemental scores, and more) for Miami Central in 2011 was a D, after having been a C in 2010. The 2012 grade returned to C, but the specific test results were mixed, at best. Interestingly, Miami Central's first grade higher than F was the 2009 test, before any involvement in Race to the Top turnaround programs. [22]

Students meeting reading standards went up slightly (16 percent in 2010, 16 percent in 2011, and 19 percent in 2012), while math performance plummeted (56 percent, 47 percent, 28 percent, in the same years). Student growth seems to have improved some over the same period. The percentage of students who showed growth in reading was 40 percent, 34 percent, and 57 percent in the same years. The math trend went in the other direction—down 74 percent, 59 percent, and 47 percent. The data are reported in such a way that determining size of the growth either for individual students or for the whole group remains unclear.

Such results do not give clear indication of a dramatically successful turnaround. In deference to the Race to the Top program, however, one might argue that the net effects of the turnaround program will take longer to register. Unfortunately, short media, electoral, and funding cycles make waiting for long-term results a politically difficult expectation to meet.

The so-called turnaround (School Improvement Grants [SIGs]) money typically comes in three-year packages. During this time, the grants stimulate significant political jockeying—first to get them, then to show that they work, and when they run out, to deflect blame about teaching positions lost because the money dried up.

In short, the money politicizes. Three middle schools in Tacoma, Washington, won SIGs at the same time as Miami Central. Upon getting the grants everyone was excited for the extra money and the promise of a brighter future. Three years later, when the money ran out, political backbiting about budgeting replaced the sense of shared commitment and enthusiasm. Along the way, the three middle schools in question showed growth ranging from little to mixed. [23]

While four examples do not prove a pattern, the story arc is all too familiar. The heightened political and social expectations created by the kinds of discussions described here prove difficult to meet, even with the extra money from the high-profile programs.

The whole process starts with enthusiasm and promise, with attendant media attention, followed by broad general claims about performance, accompanied by data reflecting mixed results, and ends with local frustration when the external program (in this case, SIG money) runs out. By the time the educational outcomes are discernible, the political actors have scored their points and moved on, leaving the local participants who want to really work on their schools in even greater frustration following from the heightened expectations that the political actors had earlier created and stoked.[24]

This brief survey is meant to highlight the nature and tone of the discussions about education and schools. We have seen that national status trumps local in these conversations, as both parents and teachers have diminished voice and status in the broader conversation. Further, people and groups who really have little role in the education debates can establish a presence by going national. Parent groups know it, and so does Bill Gates (among others).

To be fair to Gates, he does qualify his conclusions with the acknowledgment that "we know that of all the variables under a school's control, the single most decisive factor in student achievement is excellent teaching."[25] He is completely right. The problem in our social conversation arises from the fact that we take too little account of the qualification, "of all the variables under a school's control." If it turns out that the variables under a school's control contribute only a small amount to a child's educational outcomes, then so much energy and money directed the way that it currently is might be ill spent.

Clearly, schools as institutions and teachers as individuals have an impact on students. Just as clearly, though, they both have different kinds of impact on different kinds of students. Students bring widely varying intellectual, emotional, and motivational packages to school with them, yet we discuss schools as if children are blank slates, waiting to be written upon with a thoroughly transformative experience that will make every child as capable as every other child.

It remains unclear we should even want such uniformity, which is immaterial anyway—we cannot really achieve it.

Schools, of course, do bear some responsibility for the inability to smooth out the widely disparate educational outcomes. We turn now to the ways that schools as bureaucratic organizations find it difficult to meet the specific needs of such a wide range of student needs, and thereby raise political complications for themselves in so doing.

NOTES

1. Amy Chua, *Battle Hymn of the Tiger Mother* (New York: Penguin, 2011).
2. Amy Chua. "Why Chinese Mothers are Superior," *The Wall Street Journal*, January 8, 2011. http://online.wsj.com/article/SB10001424052748704111504576059713528698754.html.
3. Maureen Corrigan, "Tiger Mothers: Raising Children the Chinese Way," *National Public Radio: Books*, January 11, 2011. http://www.npr.org/2011/01/11/132833376/tiger-mothers-raising-children-the-chinese-way.
4. Kim Wong Keltner, *Tiger Babies Strike Back: How I Was Raised by a Tiger Mom but Could Not Be Turned to the Dark Side* (New York: William Morrow Paperbacks, 2013).
5. Amanda Sheaffer, "Letter to Students from a Torn Teacher," *EdWeek*, April 4, 2011. http://www.edweek.org/tm/articles/2011/04/04/lettertesting.html.
6. Allison Pearson, "The Discipline of a Chinese Mother," *The Telegraph*, January 27, 2012. www.telegraph.co.uk/women/mother-tongue/familyadvice/9041280/The-discipline-of-a-Chinese-mother.html.
7. See, among several others, Ronald Slavin, Nancy Karweit, and Barbara Wasik, *Preventing Early School Failure: Research, Policy, and Practice* (Needham Heights, MA: Allyn & Bacon, 1994).
8. Parents Across America, "Who We Are." http://parentsacrossamerica.org/who-we-are/.
9. In G-mail's new Inbox arrangement, in which mail is categorized as Primary (personal), Promotions, and Social, the PAA newsletter gets deposited in Promotions.
10. Parents Across America, "Confessions of a Bad Teacher: Buy the Book." Last modified August 15, 2013. http://parentsacrossamerica.org/confessions-bad-teacher-buy-book/.
11. National Parent Teacher Association, "National Parent Teacher Association." http://www.pta.org/.
12. Start School Later, "Health, Safety and Equity in Education." http://www.startschoollater.net/index.html.
13. Patrick McGuinn, "Fight Club," *EDUCATIONnext*, 12, no. 3 (2012), educationnext.org/fight-club/.
14. *Primary Sources: America's Teachers on America's Schools*. (Manuscript, The Bill & Melinda Gates Foundation, 2010). http://www.scholastic.com/primarysources/pdfs/Scholastic_Gates_0310.pdf.
15. For a physiological explanation of why and empirical evidence of effects, see Po Bronson and Ashley Merryman, *NurtureShock: New Thinking About Children* (New York: Twelve, 2009), chap. 2.
16. Washington state has them. Find them at Office of the Superintendent of Public Instruction, "OSPI-Developed Performance Assessments for the Arts." http://www.k12.wa.us/arts/PerformanceAssessments/default.aspx.
17. Karla Scoon Reid, "Family Engagement in Education Act Introduced in Congress," *K-12 Parents and the Public* (blog), July 17, 2013, http://blogs.edweek.org/edweek/parentsandthepublic/2013/07/family_engagement_in_education_act_introduced_in_congress.html.
18. Louis Menand, "Today's Assignment," *The New Yorker*, December 17, 2012. http://www.newyorker.com/talk/comment/2012/12/17/121217taco_talk_menand.
19. Malcolm Gladwell, *Outliers: The Story of Success* (New York: Little, Brown & Co., 2008).
20. Bill Gates, "How teacher development could revolutionize our schools," *The Washington Post*, February 28, 2011. http://www.washingtonpost.com/wp-dyn/content/article/2011/02/27/AR2011022702876.html?nav=hcmoduletmv.
21. The following discussion about Miami Central Senior High School comes from Rich Phillips, "Miami school's turnaround wins Obama's attention," *CNN*, March 4, 2011. http://www.cnn.com/2011/US/03/04/obama.miami.school/index.html.
22. All of Miami Central Senior High School score data was retrieved at the Florida Department of Education's School Accountability Report—Florida Department of Education, "Florida School Grades." Accessed August 1, 2013. http://schoolgrades.fldoe.org/, a web site filled with documents which are themselves rich in organizational complexity. As of this writing, Miami Central's 2013 grade was still pending.

23. For detailed scores, see "The Tale of Turnaround in Three Tacoma Schools, or Not," *Speaking of Education* (blog), November 20, 2013.

24. For a general overview, see www.thenewstribune.com/2013/07/21/2687788/despite-better-performance-jason.html and www.thenewstribune.com/2013/07/21/2687782/class-dismissed-clock-runs-out.html.

25. www.washingtonpost.com/wp-dyn/content/article/2011/02/27/AR2011022702876.html

Chapter Four

Organizational Culture and Social Expectations

Borrowing on organization theory, this chapter explains how the very institutional arrangements and the culture created thereby work against schools meeting the social expectations of them. For instance, schools cannot really be a "collaborative community" of "harmony in diversity" when so much of the procedures and processes of school emphasize the maximization of the individual selves.

In 1956, William Whyte published *The Organization Man.*[1] In this vastly influential book, Whyte describes and explains how Americans were increasingly gravitating to work in large organizations and live in comfortable suburbs. He points out that while both might be stifling of expressive creativity, they were each safe and enduring.

Contemporary reflections on the book tend toward concerns about the inuring effects of bureaucratized life, or lamentations about how fear is motivating more Americans to follow these malignant (or at least, maligned) patterns. The insights from this pathbreaking analysis of bureaucratic life reverberate in our contemporary evaluation of education—understanding organizations and bureaucratic conduct helps us understand important aspects of the current situation that schools find themselves in.

Schools, after all, are bureaucratic organizations. Further, each successively higher level of the education hierarchy—school boards, state offices of education, and the federal department of education—is composed as a bureaucratic organization. In other words, successive layers of bureaucracy—from the local school all the way up to Washington, DC—constitute the system we call education. Teaching, or the process of learning, on the other hand, is highly relational and idiosyncratic to each individual teacher and

47

learner. What Johnny needs will differ from what Jonathan needs, and Joanna requires something still different.

That's the rub. Individual students have individual educational needs, and respond to educational stimuli differently. Schools are organized, however, as highly structured and institutionalized organizations that function most effectively when they are able to repeat a set of predictably routine procedures.

Look, for instance, at the school in your neighborhood. If it was built in the last ten years, it will bear striking resemblance to all the other schools built in the same time period. Look for a shed roof, numerous or expansive windows, some amount of exposed cinder block and a pleasingly warm—and usually muted—palate of several colors, usually coded to match the wing or grade level housed therein.

Today's schools are designed to maximize natural light, but earlier somebody must have thought that school rooms with only the smallest of windows were desirable. Furthermore, you can likely find but few schools that transcend the kind of linear, square, and institutional layout and appointment so typical of contemporary school buildings. The similarities among schools go beyond structural likeness, though.

These buildings are designed to accommodate several hundred to a couple thousand human beings of varying ages, all in the work of getting their education. The smooth functioning of these buildings relies on bureaucratic procedure, and rules are foundational to that. Stop in for the first day of school at any of these buildings and you will get treated to numerous reviews of rules.

In a middle and high school, each classroom will have a set of rules. Each grade level might have a set of particular expectations (executed as rules) for students in that grade level. On top of these are the school rules governing behavior in the common areas and aspects of school life. The district further adds certain broad policies, like prohibitions against bullying.

Each school day is also organized around particular patterns. Bells signal the specific and routine time for much of the day's movements. Lunch is always at precisely the same time, which for some students might be quite early. Activities and movement outside these routine patterns are governed by procedures granting such privileges to students. Students, of course, find this oppressive and "boring," while the adults demand it for the sake of keeping an order that makes the day's work of teaching and learning go more smoothly.

At one level, the rules keep order so that the hundreds of students can live and learn together more effectively. Following the standardization process (see chapter 5), the variety of learning goals and expectations also boil down to a set of routines that the school implements. Since the primary goal is to get students to meet the standard on the annual test, school staff are incentivized to emphasize the relevant component elements of each standardized test, and they create rules they think will improve the prospects of doing so.

Teachers are perfectly familiar with precisely the kinds of things that will be examined in the spring, and this inflects their teaching. This inflection is institutionalized in the "best practice" that calls for teachers to post the target standards in their rooms, so they and their students can always focus on the standards goal. Research indicates that people learn a thing better when they are told the goal beforehand, but at the same time the posting of ten overarching standardized goals can also narrow the focus of the work.

Teachers would be foolish to neglect this focus, though, especially since the test—the standardized test—is so predictable. Every language arts teacher knows not only that questions on main idea, inference, summary, author's purpose, and so forth will follow the non-fiction passages, but also exactly what the questions look like. Fiction passages, math, and science follow their set of routine patterns.

A teacher does not have to intentionally "teach to the test" to be shaped by the expectations derived from these routines. Rather, the test nudges school staff to teach in particular ways. Indeed, teachers neglect this standardization of teaching to their professional peril. (We will examine this further in subsequent chapters.)

The management of schools also follows predictable routines. From procedures for entering assemblies to the time at which students may enter the building, from where students may have food to which side of the hall to walk, schools have rules to regularize behavior. Indeed, without these rules and the patterns following therefrom, the adults would be overwhelmed before the end of the first day.

From top to bottom—federal government to the school itself—bureaucratic organization and structure embody the education system. But individual people live and work in these organizations. And as in interaction with any bureaucracy, students and parents often find their needs (or their preferences) unmet by the bureaucratic routine of school. Furthermore, any student divergence from the routine must be accounted and monitored, whether it is excessive absences, or the desire to leave class to see a counselor or—most importantly—failure to meet standard on the state exam. [2]

If schools and the school system are characterized by bureaucracy and all that entails, then individuals—parents, students and, in a different way, school staff—will have some difficulty meeting goals and values particular to their specific needs and hopes. The divergence between organizational procedure and varying individual needs is much the nature of bureaucratic life.

We can see this difficulty regarding education in the character of the social conversation about schools. National and expert discussants set the agenda and shape the debate. Even what appear to be discussions that include locals are shaped by insiders and are held in the halls of institutions far from local school districts. As before, a wide variety of examples illustrate the difficulties and complexity that arise when people interact with bureaucracies.

A few years ago, Washington (state) newspapers reported on a particular lobbying event, regarding education.[3] The specifics are immaterial—the pattern of views and expectations tells all. One report of this event was called "WA education advocates lobby for school reform."[4] The title misleads, though, as both the article and the lobbying relied on a lot of clichés and generated more confusion than clarity.

In any case, this lobbying effort precisely captures the pattern of the social conversation we are considering here. The education advocates who participated in the meeting, for instance, filled specific institutional roles in the education system. The people named in the article include "education leaders," like the state superintendent and a parent from Tacoma. Teachers and teacher representatives, the story says, were absent.

Everyone described in the review of the event was an education advocate, from their own respective organizational perspectives. One was a mother, from the Black Education Strategy Roundtable, an advocacy group with a particular educational agenda. The state superintendent's advocacy is inflected, of course, with his organizational interest, and teachers, especially when represented by the union, have personal job interests at stake. Organizationally speaking, in other words, the superintendent, teachers, and even this particular mother are education advocates and pursuers of their self-interest. These dual roles should cause circumspection in our thinking about and response to their views.

Moreover, each participant is deemed an advocate because, in fact, they have some level of status or expertise in the politics of education. Well-informed and interested parents may only gain entry to the discussion by way of an institutional affiliation that "warrants" them having access. Teachers' access is by way of the union, which governs and shapes the teacher view.

In any case, the proposals that come out of such "advocacy" are marginal or, at best, so generic as to be meaningless: a longer school day and more credits for high school students, preschool for low-income kids, all-day kindergarten, more fairness in the way the state passes out money to schools around the state, and more money for librarians, counselors, and nurses.

No surprises there, and hardly disagreeable, except on the part of the teachers union, apparently. But little can really come of this kind of proposal in an institutional environment so thickly populated with bureaucratic conduct and interests. The real prospects for discussion are too consistently hemmed in, or at least defined, by the array of organizational actors and their interests.

We can see this at work from the most local issues all the way up to state and national arenas. The case of Miami Central Senior High highlights the national-level expression of this. In the last chapter, we examined this case as an example of the politicization of the school reform discussion. In the context of bureaucratic reality, we can see Miami Central as an example of the national education bureaucracy (and the elite who populate it) entering into and shaping the course of the conversation about education.

The lesson here is that a bureaucracy constituted to work on education issues, or to work on educating students, must do *something* toward the goal of improving education. An organizational structure created on the premise of overseeing and advancing education cannot sit by and simply let school happen.

Rather, these organizational actors must act, and they do so according to the sense of their organizational mission. In so acting—according to and by way of their organization's preferences and capacities—the organization shows its worth by its presumed salutary effect on the system and on students. This holds true from school boards to the federal Department of Education, and every bureaucratic level in between.

These bureaucracies must act, yet they face constraints in what they can realistically do. If you are a local school board, you have specific organizational tools available, so you will tend to embrace a definition of the problem that allows you to act according to what your organizational tools enable. Your action may or may not generate relevant impact, but you must be seen to do something.

A school board can only offer responses that are within its tool kit. More teachers, more pre-K interventions, cultural awareness training, and so on are possible; maintenance of effective family involvement (see the discussion of the bedtime story below) is much less so. This practical constraint on bureaucratic action results in school board members getting particularly excited to find money for three or four more pre-K teachers, or iPads for virtual letter learning, but unable to seriously affect the amount of time and engagement parents commit to their children's reading (prior to entering school), which makes a far more robust contribution to a child's educational success than more teachers or iPads.

Further, such organizational limitations can leave a school board little choice but to accept the definition and source of the problem as something within the domain of its own structure and processes. Doing so makes it substantially easier to embrace expansive programs of redress by reform or restructuring. Consider Tacoma's achievement gap issue (see below). By accepting the claim that teacher quality is the problem, the bureaucrats take on the substantial project (which bureaucrats need) of transforming the schools.

Consequently, more productive responses, for instance, stimulating better parent involvement, or even maintenance of stable families even more generally, are simply dropped. This is fine enough with the educational bureaucracy—those are not projects they would want to be involved in anyway. Measurement, monitoring, tidy reporting, and so on of such things are much more complicated.

The logic of the organizationally possible applies at the other bureaucratic levels, too. In the last year of her governorship of Washington, Christine Gregoire proposed a substantial reorganization of the school bureaucracy . . . at the state level. She hoped to put all state education, preschool through college, under the direction of one state agency. Currently, K-12 and higher education have their own organizational identity—along with twelve other agencies working on education—in the capital.

The plan met predictable resistance from the agency leaders who would be subsumed into the new organization, whose head would answer directly to the governor. Also predictable was the governor's rhetoric explaining the plan. "We know that learning starts at birth and continues throughout one's life. . . . It's time we reflect the reality of that by bringing our education efforts . . . into a single, focused education agency,"[5] she said, as if it makes obvious sense that one agency at the state level would clearly do a better a job of the whole educational project.

The plan did not come to pass before Gregoire's governorship concluded, so the reconstructed organizational flow chart presented at the time of the proposal is now unavailable at any state of Washington web site. As is so often true of supposedly substantial organizational restructuring, the new flow chart appeared to be about as complex as the chart it was replacing. Obviously, flow charts say little about how the practical political and organizational realities play out, but complicated flow charts do portend bureaucratic wrangling, and attendant complexity.

More importantly, such a bureaucratic reorganization and any resulting organizational complexity does not have much real impact on what a teacher does in his or her classroom each day. Nobody should seriously think that any child's education is going to be tangibly affected by either the changes the governor proposes or the state superintendent's counterclaims for organizational continuity. Such proposals are much more about authority and resources, at the bureaucratic level under consideration, and much less about specific classroom conduct.

Consider an all too typical discussion about a failing student. The conversation might start with one staff member making a comment like this, "[Student] has been struggling academically for many years. We [the school] need to come up with an action plan to help him be successful!"[6] Staff members involved in this discussion will look "down" the hierarchy—the relationship between student and school staff—when considering supports for that student. Nobody would look "up" the hierarchy, no matter how it's organized, to a bureaucrat who spends so much time wrangling the bureaucratic structure so far removed from the school and classroom.

The nexus of upper-level bureaucrats and insider elite thinking also pushes its way down to the local level by way of consultants (typically, not local to the districts hiring them), who dramatically shape local discussions. One of the most obvious and common expressions of this is the hiring of headhunting firms to identify prospective candidates for high-level district administration roles. Consultants also contribute to a district's work on the very small details, though. Much teacher professional development, for instance, is undertaken by consultants who are supposed to be experts in some facet of education, presumably that facet the district is eager to bolster.

Districts also hire consultants to analyze substantive areas of a district's performance, and make recommendations about changes and improvements. The latter part is key. Consultants are not hired to simply give a pithy analysis of a district. Rather, the district thinks it has a problem to solve and the consultant will help. Consultants, then, have substantive incentive to see problems (indeed, the district highlights those problems for the consultant) and to offer solutions.

A consultant really would not have much of a business for very long, if he/she found that district's problems were not solvable with the tools that the consultant can offer. The prospects are dim, for instance, for an educational consultancy that says to a school district, "Don't worry . . . you'll have a certain amount of normal failure, no matter what you do."

Educational consultants, in other words, are motivated to find clear and soluble problems, and in so doing, they oversimplify complex circumstances. If the issue in view is small and politically insignificant, probably only the insiders (school staff) will have to worry about the consultant's recommendations or findings. If the issue is significant and politically charged, many other locals outsiders—parents and interest groups—get activated. The achievement gap is one such issue, and it has stirred controversy in the education establishment for years. Here's how it has played out in the Tacoma School District.

Like many districts, Tacoma experiences a gap in the test score achievements between Caucasian students and both African American and Hispanic students. To give just one example, eighth grade standardized test pass rates for 2012 are shown in the table below.

Clearly, both African Americans and Hispanics pass at a substantially lower rate than Caucasian students. Furthermore, African American and Hispanic students pass at essentially the exact same rates. [7]

This problem was important and substantial enough that the district hired a consultant to evaluate the sources and suggest likely solutions. But the consultant's initial assessment, submitted in 2009, framed the issue different-

	Reading	Math	Science
Caucasian	66.3	46.7	66.1
African American	39.7	22.1	33.2
Hispanic	40.1	23.5	35.4

ly, thereby opening the door to significant politicization. First, the report is entitled Addressing the Achievement Gap for African American Students in Tacoma Public Schools,[8] and it mentions Hispanics only twice—once in 1970 census data offered as part of the background, and once to note that Hispanics have higher GPAs than African Americans.

Second, the report goes on to conclude that the achievement gap for African American students is caused primarily by:

- Inequitable distribution of skilled and experienced teachers

and secondary causes of the achievement gap are:

- Inter-generational poverty
- Families/communities who are not able to support or adequately advocate for their children and often are not welcomed by the education system.[9]

This report reflects the highly charged social environment these schools live in. Besides apparently dismissing the Hispanic achievement gap, the report's author finds primary causes unsupportable by the evidence, as the author even acknowledges in saying, "The degree to which quality teachers are available to African American students in Tacoma schools could not be determined with the available information."[10]

Furthermore, to claim that poverty and the decreased family support that typically attends poverty is of secondary importance flies in the face of the overwhelming bulk of education scholarship. A UNESCO overview of education and poverty, for instance, summarizes the relationship between the two very clearly: "Educational research has consistently found home background (socio-economic status) to be an important determinant of educational outcomes."[11]

It is unimportant here to determine whether the local politics shaped the report or vice versa—most likely the two were mutually reinforcing. The point is that local political actors pick up these ideas and incorporate them into their views and values about education and their local schools. In so doing, the local discussion of schools shifts to demands for institutional change and away from relationship-building.

In the case of Tacoma, one can easily follow the virtual paper trail. Following the release of the consultant's report, a coalition of interest groups joined together in one umbrella organization,[12] which created an agenda reflecting the findings and suggestions from the same report. Indeed, the group's web site offers a link to the report, as well as to a series of proposals created following from that report.

The politicization arose from the advocacy group's calls for solutions that remain unsupported by the findings. Even though the consultant acknowledges a lack of evidence about the quality of teachers that African American students are getting, she and the advocacy group both put the onus on teachers, and call for a teacher evaluation protocol (student test scores constituting a significant portion) and increased cultural competency training to close the achievement gap.

Along the way, they offer little evidence that either cultural training or more elaborate teacher evaluations generate higher student achievement. Indeed, the advocacy group's web site calls the reforms "common sense," and offers a link to "research,"[13] which consists of five documents, mostly surveys and reports . . . done by other consultants.

The research on cultural competence is particularly lacking. Most organizations and articles that support cultural competence offer extensive resources—which they call research—about what cultural competence is and admonitions about why it is the right thing to do. Evidence of cultural competence programs' effects on learning outcomes remains largely intuitive, not data based. Washington state's Office of the Superintendent of Public Instruction offers this "research" on cultural competence.[14]

Online Articles

Understanding Culture and Cultural Responsiveness
Culturally Responsive Pedagogy and Practice
Culturally Responsive Classroom Descriptors
Culturally Responsive Lesson Plan Descriptors
Culturally Responsive Resources
Massachusetts Educational Leadership Alliance
Closing the Achievement Gap: Oregon's Bold Plan in Educational Leadership
Washington 2008 Achievement Gap Studies
Supporting Teachers of English Language Learners
Cultural Competence for Teachers
Common Misconceptions about Cultural Competence
Booklist provided by ReachOut for New Futures

Books

Courageous Conversations about Race

Strategies and Lessons for Culturally Responsive Teaching: A Primer for
K-12 Teachers
Classroom Instruction that Works with English Language Learners
Improving Multicultural Education: Lessons from the Intergroup Education Movement
Culturally Proficient Coaching: Supporting Educators to Create Equitable Schools

Lesson plans, resources, and how-to overviews might be helpful, but they do not prove research-based best practice.

The debate over test-based teacher evaluations is more complicated, but plenty of serious research has been done on the topic. The Economic Policy Institute published one of the more extensive and widely cited studies of the issue.[15] They point out various technical and statistical difficulties of such programs, to be sure.

The more serious problem, however, is the slew of unintended negative consequences, like a narrowed curriculum, decreased teacher collaboration, and disincentive to work with needier students that follow. In the end, the authors counsel caution when using score-based evaluations. In other words, evaluations based on test scores will affect the choices teachers and schools make about what they teach, and that won't always be for the best.

In short, there is no magic bullet for fixing education. The steady and consistent building of trusting relationships among the community, families, school administration, school staff, and students will make education more effective, but that's a prospect complicated in its own way. This relationship-building could follow from a serious conversation addressing the kinds of questions above.

In a social environment, however, where data are sometimes demanded, and other times intuition reigns, politicization gains a foothold, and trust-building conversations become less and less likely. Schools and teachers have to fight, then, an impulse to turn inward, to retrench to their own specialized understanding and analysis. Being bureaucratic organizations, with some measure of interest in protecting their organizational status and budget, that's not easy to do.

The dearth of magic bullets does not mean, however, that education leaders and reformers cease searching for them. In what sometimes seems like desperation, districts and schools almost constantly adjust and change structures, curriculum, even staff in pursuit of better performance. Sometimes, these efforts can seem almost comical. For instance, several neighboring school districts in the South Puget Sound (south of Seattle) area considered—at the same time—reorganizing their schools for the middle years. Along the way, the notion of universal "best practices" took another confusing turn.

Two school districts had been using what is called the junior high model (grades seven–nine in the same building, ten–twelve at the high school) and considered moving (one actually did switch) to the middle school model (grades six–eight in one building, nine–twelve at the high school).[16] The third district uses the middle school model, but considered a move to the junior high model.[17] One district (maybe two, depending on who does what), in other words, is quitting best practice and moving to second-best practice, unless, of course, we allow local variation and idiosyncrasy. Standardization and bureaucratization do not allow such, though.

Herein reflects the conceptual and practical muddledness of "best practice"—it's too hard to determine, measure, and evaluate when you're talking about the widely diverse, even divergent, needs of such large numbers of people engaged in such a wide range of different tasks. The difficulty heightens—because the complexity increases—if we try to talk about an education "system," writ large.

If we say, however, that different districts, schools, rooms, and so forth may have best practices that differ from their neighbors, then we are implicitly acknowledging that we have less of an education system than most experts (national insiders) seem to assume. Either way, education is complicated, sloppy, expensive, and local.

Moreover, implementing something called best practices implies a goal. We can fairly say, "These are the best practices to achieve that goal." But, in pursuit of a goal we make choices about tradeoffs, and opportunities foregone, when dedicating ourselves to the preferred goal. Too often, though, claiming "best practice" in the broad and general way serves as an organizational trump card played in discussions about curriculum or policy or procedure. Acknowledgment of tradeoffs falls away from such rhetorical thrusts.

If we were to say "raise the test scores" is the primary goal, for instance, then we could identify a best practice to accomplish that. But we live in some degree of denial that we elevate (almost reify) test scores, and in so doing allow ourselves to also pretend that we can identify the best practices for everything else, then drive toward all those other goals, too, all without ever facing the ways that those different goals might conflict with the myriad other goals we maintain. In so doing, we increase the organizational, pedagogical, and social complexity of education and of schools.

Finally, best practice also submits to certain philosophical and moral principles. Choosing to expend significant portions of finite resources on programs for underachieving students may be a socially good and desirable thing, but it does reduce the availability of resources for other programs. Or, in a less emotionally charged example, cash incentives given to students for performance on the standardized tests violates philosophical commitments about both education for its own sake and delayed gratification in youngsters.

The organizational difficulties of pursuing supposedly best practices muddle school culture and climate in less obvious ways, too. Everyone agrees that education is based in some degree on relationships. General school climate, discipline, academic performance, and so on are all better when the adults have good relationships with their charges. The too-pithy saying that "they have to know you care before they care what you know" reflects this need for relationship.

At the same time, as we have already seen, schools and school districts are bureaucratic organizations, which, of course, like to save money and minimize their exposure to unnecessary risks. This is why it should not surprise anyone that a school district would seek the 5 percent discount on its liability insurance that some insurance companies offer when all district staff take something called "boundary invasion" (regarding relationships between adults and students) training. Unfortunately, too often such "trainings" are quick, check-off-that-box meetings where the conclusion is something oblique like "be smart, don't do anything that could even be construed as social, rather than instructional, with your students."

One of the most unnerving and risky places to interact with students is, of course, the web, particularly on social networks. So an official district suggestion that staff avoid social media connections with current or former students until ten years after they have left school, while a long time, makes some sense.

So imagine the dilemma a teacher might feel when, hours after hearing the "ten years" directive, he/she receives in the school mail a magazine called *Teaching Tolerance*, that edition of which includes an article called, "Your Students Love Social Media . . . And So Can You: Want to engage students? Meet them on society's newest public square." A psychologist cited in the article says this, "From my perspective, this new technology is all a very positive thing. Social media has totally changed the communication model. This is so empowering."[18]

The new technologies are empowering, indeed. But this expert seems to neglect the all too evident empowerment for negative inherent in these technologies. Every technology, and the institutional arrangements it creates, offers opportunity for both good and bad, which is precisely why a district's insurance company prefers that teachers stay away from it with students.

Relationships bear with them certain kinds of risk, but district leadership and risk managers prefer not to take on the particular kinds of risks that attend social media relationships, and they do prefer 5 percent discounts on their insurance. All reasonable enough, but try to write a "best practice" rule out of those divergent expectations and goals.

It remains unclear that any real academic benefit derives from social media contact anyway. A program of text message encouragement[19] to students in Oklahoma City Public Schools found students self-reported greater effort in their work, but there were "no detectable changes in academic achievement."[20] The students had a better attitude about school, but they didn't perform any better in school. Social media may make relationships better and richer, but the attendant risks are not worth the non-existent academic payoff.

We have taken a broad snapshot of the educational hierarchy at various levels. We turn now to the smallest, most intimate level in the hierarchy of education—the family. Turns out, families have learning styles and cultures, almost like the patterning inherent in bureaucratic organizations. These patterns pass from parents to children, and, as you might imagine, not all styles fit well with the schools' expectations or procedures.

In a landmark study, Shirley Brice Heath described three different levels of parental engagement with their children's learning, particularly reading.[21] Examining the process and conduct of the bedtime story in families, Heath found that one group of parents (let's call them Readers) begins reading with their children very early, provides a wide variety of reading material, and teaches (consciously or not) that there is much to "take away" from reading. These parents show, demonstrate, and teach their children to interact with the text by making inferences, drawing conclusions, evaluating context, making comparisons, and so forth.

These are the kinds of so-called higher level skills that appear on every standardized test out there. In other words, school and the testing process are organized around the kinds of processes that Readers are instilling in their children from an early age. Furthermore, school is designed—structurally and philosophically—by people who are good at this, and who think this reading/learning process is good and right. (Ask a teacher . . . nearly all of them will say they were "good at" school.) Consequently, kids from this kind of background will be much more likely to succeed at school than will kids from Group 2.

Group 2 parents (call them Ambivalents) read less to their children and tend to be more ambivalent about the material. Their interactions tend to involve more of the recall/recapitulation process, and the higher level reading skills are engaged less deeply. Children in this group are less likely to grow up thinking there is a breadth and depth of worthwhile material in a piece of reading, and less likely to have the skills to find that breadth and depth.

While they are less likely to be as effective at reading as the children of Readers, they can certainly strengthen their reading abilities to the point of being highly successful in school environments, which are better suited to Readers. Indeed, the current schooling model may be best suited to supporting growth in these students.

Group 3 parents (Non-Readers) do not read much at all to their children and tend to see much less value in the process of reading or in the reading material than do Readers, or even Ambivalents. The children of these type of parents are the least likely to be successful in the reading-driven elements of school.

Heath makes several observations about these groups of parents and children, including that each does have a literary experience of life, they just access and express that experience differently. Further, parents in all three groups undoubtedly want and hope for their children to be well educated. The study makes clear that the latter two groups of parents may be less certain about the best things for enhancing their children's learning prospects in a school environment.

Since schools are overwhelmingly set up in ways that play to Readers' strengths, Heath's study demands that we think about the need to adjust pedagogy for the variety of students that enter the schoolhouse door. One could make the moral claim that schools privilege one group (Readers) over another (Ambivalents and Non-Readers) and are therefore unfairly constructed. But we need not make even that stark an argument to say that the distribution of these three different kinds of students across a school makes for a more complicated educational environment. This is true for several reasons.

First, to the degree that one classroom has a mix of these different students, a teacher essentially has three different kinds of teaching tasks, a difficulty which intensifies in the higher grades where the academic divergences widen. Readers who have been keeping up with grade-level learning expectations will be in a very different place for the whole of their academic experience than will Non-Readers, who will likely fall further behind with each passing year. Ambivalents are the interesting uncertainty in the situation—over the years they will likely go in various directions.

Second, the teaching of reading mechanics (decoding, fluency, etc.) is far from the most important aspect of literacy. The article points this out, but it can't be reiterated enough. The differences among these three groups of students also demand, therefore, a more serious evaluation of the "Every child can learn" trope. The three groups will need different kinds of supports from early on, and they will likely learn differently throughout their academic careers.

From this, we need to think about several questions. Can Non-Readers learn in the same way that Readers do? Is school constructed to reach one group more than the others, and to what effect on those other groups? Should school be constructed in some other way? Should we consider, for example, classes and curriculum fit to variations in learning of the three different groups? Should and can we transform Non-Readers into Readers? If so, how? Or should we try to create more work and learning opportunities engaging Ambivalents and Non-Readers on their own terms? If so, at what opportunity costs? Is the current model or structure or organization of schooling adequate to this diversification?

Third—the elephant in the room—is the standardized testing process inclined in favor of one or two of the groups and against the others? Would it be reasonable to figure out a different metric and learning goal for the different groups of kids? The next two chapters cover the standardized test, so for now the answers are simply Yes and Yes.

Fourth, and perhaps most importantly, is there some way to engage Ambivalents and Non-Reader parents earlier, and get them to help their kids see the value of the reading and learning process? There is only so much a teacher can do to reconstruct a child's enculturation toward reading and learning, so getting more done earlier (at home) will be better for a child. This set of questions, of course, embraces school structured as a Readers' world, which may not be the best course, philosophically, but remains the organizational and political reality of what school is today.

The scope of this book does not cover all those questions. The point here is that families, which create at least three different "styles" of reader/student, send their children into bureaucratic organizations for their education. Those bureaucratic organizations, which differ in significant ways and so do not constitute much more than a loose "system," have sets of routines and patterns that do not work the same for each style of student, let alone each specific child. In other words, bureaucratic organizations educating children is a complicated—and sloppy and expensive—business.

In the last two chapters, we have taken snapshots of various organizational, social, and political realities of education. This review may be too narrow and specific, rather than broad and general—fair enough, depending on the objective in taking this picture. Here, we have tried to get the flavor of the myriad conversations going on in multitudinous places at multiple bureaucratic locations and levels. The point has been to discern the nuance and complexity of the conversations about education. The seeming randomness is the point, since, for teachers, much of this conversation is effectively meaningless.

Indeed, for many (but not all) classroom teachers, both the national and local discussions fundamentally miss the point because neither really takes much account of what a school and its classrooms are really like. Or, more to the point, little discussion takes account of what those specific teachers' schools and rooms are like. Understanding that there is such nearly infinite variability of schools and rooms has been one of the main objectives of this book.

Further, we have considered schools and the school system—from the federal Department of Education to the family—as bureaucratic organizations. Each level of the organizational hierarchy enters the discussion about education with particular views and values. While organizational actors higher up the hierarchy (national insiders) focus on the national system, families (local outsiders) and school staff (local insiders) pursue more specific and particular goals.

The needs, hopes, and claims that each group makes differ significantly. Further, as those expectations become institutionalized into a bureaucratic structure (especially above the level of the family), the complexity mounts. Bureaucratic organizations function according to routines, by which they create—both intentionally and unintentionally—performance patterns. Patterns of conduct based on different, sometimes divergent, goals will yield some degree of disagreement and uncertainty up and down the hierarchy as each group struggles with the way that the other bureaucratic actors and structures respond to them and to each other.

Ideally, the standardized test process could be a procedure upon which all could all agree, and around which could form a consensus on how to measure student performance, teacher effectiveness, and the overall success of the school system. The test could be, in other words, the antidote to this organizational complexity. In the next two chapters we will examine why this has not been the case.

NOTES

1. William Whyte, *The Organization Man* (New York: Simon & Schuster, 1956).
2. In Washington state, a student who fails to meet standard on any portion of the standardized test is supposed to have a teacher-parent conference, at which a plan for improvement is developed with the student. In theory, this paperwork is filed at the state superintendent's office.
3. Donna Gordon Blankinship, "WA education advocates lobby for school reform," *The Seattle Times*, April 15, 2009. http://seattletimes.com/html/localnews/2009065462_apwaxgreducationdollars.html.
4. Ibid.
5. Linda Shaw, "Gregoire wants just one state education agency," *The Seattle Times*, January 5, 2011. http://seattletimes.com/html/localnews/2013850318_edfunding06m.html.
6. Private communication among teachers and staff regarding a middle school student.
7. For further detail, see Office of the Superintendent of Public Instruction, "Washington State Report Card." http://reportcard.ospi.k12.wa.us/waslCurrent.aspx?groupLevel=District&schoolId=188&reportLevel=District&orgLinkId=188&yrs=2011-12&gradeLevelId=8&waslCategory=1&year=2011-12&chartType=1.
8. Thelma Jackson, *Addressing the Achievement Gap for African American Students in Tacoma Public Schools.* (Manuscript, 2009), http://www.tacoma.k12.wa.us/information/departments/assessment/Achievement Gap Documents/Addressing the Achievement Gap Report.pdf.
9. Ibid., p. 13.
10. Ibid., p. 15
11. Servaas van der Berg, *Poverty and Education* (Manuscript. International Institute for Educational Planning, 2008), http://www.iiep.unesco.org/fileadmin/user_upload/Info_Services_Publications/pdf/2009/EdPol10.pdf, p. 100.
12. Vibrant Schools Tacoma Coalition, "Community Voices for Student Success." http://vibrantschooltacoma.org/.
13. Vibrant Schools Tacoma Coalition, "Research." http://vibrantschoolstacoma.org/?page_id=6.

14. Office of the Superintendent of Public Instruction, "Eliminating the Gaps." http://www. k12.wa.us/CISL/EliminatingtheGaps/CulturalCompetence/Research.aspx.

15. Richard Rothstein et al., *Problems with the use of student test scores to evaluate teachers.* (Manuscript, Economic Policy Institute, 2010), http://www.epi.org/publication/bp278/.

16. Sara Schilling, "Bethel school panel votes to recommend switch to middle school format," *The News Tribune,* December 17, 2010. http://www.thenewstribune.com/2010/12/17/1468619/bethel-board-seeks-change.html.

17. Debbie Caffazzo, "Junior High Return Sought in Tacoma," *The News Tribune,* September 27, 2010. http://www.thenewstribune.com/2010/09/27/1357804/junior-high-return-sought. html.

18. Camille Jackson, "Your Students Love Social Media . . . and So Can You," *Teaching Tolerance,* 39, no. Spring (2011), http://www.tolerance.org/magazine/number-39-spring-2011/feature/your-students-love-social-media-and-so-can-you.

19. Encouraging messages included: "Each year, H.S. dropouts make $21,023. College graduates make $58,613. Do the math. (United States Census Bureau 2011)" and "High school dropouts are more than three times as likely to be unemployed as college graduates" (Bureau of Labor Statistics 2011). Persuasive examples included: "People don't look down on someone for being too educated" and "Graduates never regret staying in school, but dropouts often regret leaving it."

20. Ronald Fryer, Jr., "Information and Student Achievement: Evidence from a Cellular Phone Experiment." (Unpublished working paper, Harvard University, 2013), p. 25.

21. Shirley Brice Heath, "What No Bedtime Story Means: Narrative Skills at Home and School," *Language in Society,* 11, no. 1 (1982): 49-76.

Chapter Five

Standardized Testing Creates a Culture of Complexity

As technical people, we are apt to be preoccupied with scores, not competence.
—Neil Postman [1]

In this chapter, we review the standardized test process to discover that the tests change consistently, the educational goals (standards) may not reflect the main purpose of education, and evaluating either students or teachers by way of test scores is neither clear nor helpful.

The standardized test process creates a special kind of "choice environment," to borrow the language of the insightful *Nudge*. Schools make (or have made for them) choices about how to undertake teaching and what "learning" needs to be done and by whom. As Thaler and Sunstein [2] consistently point out, a choice environment affects us by incentivizing and motivating certain kinds of actions.

Choice environments are not neutral—they shape outcomes by encouraging certain choices and actions while discouraging others. And so it is with the standardized test. To really understand contemporary education, then, we must discern and evaluate the incentive structures that the test creates and how the resultant incentives shape teaching and learning in a particular way.

To see this, we will consider what a standardized test is and what it measures. Along the way, we will consider the organizational realities of the standardized environment, including issues of what is at stake on test outcomes. We will also examine how standard—universal—the tests are. In the following chapter, we will look closely at some standardized tests and see that they just may not be assessing what we think they're assessing.

Standardized is one of those words that everyone uses, but few fully understand or stop to think about it. So, do a word part exercise, much like an eighth grade student of vocabulary might be compelled to do: standard means many things. The two definitions applicable to this particular context are (1) something established by authority, custom, or general consent as a model or example and (2) something set up and established by authority as a rule for the measure of quantity, weight, extent, or quality.

For purposes of this discussion, when we talk about standardized, standard means the place or point we agree to call acceptable or adequate or expected, as in "students need to meet standard"—a specific score on a performance test—in various school subjects. It can also connote a certain level of quality. "We set high standards"—levels of achievement that we expect. Obviously, we could meet standard while achieving at very low standards. . . . It depends on where we set the bar.

The *-ize* makes the noun into a verb, and *d* makes it past tense, arriving at a word that means some sort of process has been undertaken in which the acceptable level of performance has been determined. When we use the word *standardized,* then, we are using a passive voice construction to say that something has been fashioned into a form that has been connected to or made into a standard.

Questions abound in this. What has been standardized . . . the curriculum in order to make a largely objective test easier to administer, or the test in relationship to the curriculum? Have learning outcomes been routinized along the way . . . a by-product of standardization? Do students end up more standardized, then? Who does the standardizing? Who are the experts or authorities, in other words, who set the standards? Do we all generally consent to these standards? Are we sure that "meeting standard" is what we want from the educational process?

Most importantly for the discussion here, what kind of choice environment do we establish when we emphasize success on the standardized test? Economists are wont to tell us that everything comes with a price—if not a monetary cost, at least an opportunity cost, or a tradeoff. For instance, students with one elective course to fill cannot choose both band and art, so the opportunity cost of taking band is the missed art class. Since resources (in this case, time) are finite, we are routinely faced with tradeoffs.

When changing (or, reforming) the education "system," we face an array of such tradeoffs, though they are perhaps more subtle and unseen. Without taking a political or philosophical view either way, we must acknowledge, for instance, that devoting extensive teaching resources to special education, with the low teacher-student ratios, means a tradeoff—less is available for other programs. Similarly, in tough budget times, schools make choices about cutting clubs or sports. The most expensive sport—football—is one of the hardest to cut because it's so popular and high profile. To keep football would mean cutting other (and more, since they would save less than cutting football would) sports or clubs or activities. Furthermore, for each male sport cut, the school must also cut one female sport, too. The tradeoffs struck in all these decisions reflect very real opportunity costs.

So it is with the choice environment created by the reality of the standardized test. The system we are creating—primarily, a pass/fail standardized test and the promise of teacher evaluations connected to student performance on that test—nudges schools and teachers to emphasize the standards and target the students hovering around or just below the standard. Here's how:

The standards are the agglomeration of successively smaller sub-standards. Reading is divided into two strands—informational text and literature. Informational text is further divided into strands for key ideas and details, craft and structure, and integration of knowledge and ideas, each with several further sub-strands.[3]

The same kind of strand branching applies to literature, writing, speaking and listening, and language (grammar). Math, of course, is similarly broken into strands this way. Presumably, the mastery of all these individual strand standards will add up to a complete and workable understanding—knowledge and the skills to use it—as the student re-integrates all those standards/skills back into one whole, at some point.

Never mind the fact that some students will be delightful writers who want nothing to do with public speaking, while others will disarm audiences with material that shy writers produced for them. Now, fully effective education means getting every student to meet these basic standards in every strand of every subject. Short of that, education is failing.

This re-orientation has, of course, an educational philosophy of sorts embedded in it. We may no longer accept that students have very different strengths and desires. Instead, we must now make sure that everybody has an identical set of skills . . . that supposedly make them "career and college ready."

Along the way, the culture and organization of school have shifted toward standards-meeting. And if teachers and schools are going to be assessed by the numbers (percentages) of students who get over the elusive bar, then energy and emphasis will naturally move toward the level of the standards. Students who are comfortably above the standards needn't be worried over or engaged educationally. Students far below the standards . . . well, perhaps they need to be referred for special services.

What schools increasingly want is to get the so-called bubble kids (those just below the pass mark) up and over the top, into passing. More of this makes the school's test pass rate go up, and the school is deemed more successful. High-achieving kids scoring even higher on the test means nothing under the incentive structure we are creating with standardized tests. Neither does fantastic improvement that falls just short of passing.

In short, the standardized test environment nudges schools and teachers to spend more educational energy "around the standard." Among all other concerns, this also means we had better set good, effective, and consistent standards. Unfortunately, it's not clear we do any of this. The rest of this chapter and the next will elaborate this further.

The word *standard* also means "usual or customary," as in regular. In the context of testing, this should mean routine or universal, as in the test remains constant in form, design, structure, and so forth. If the test changes too much, too frequently, comparison across years becomes more difficult. Testing specialists seem to understand this need of consistency. Note the answer of one state education bureaucracy to this:

Frequently Asked Question—Are state testing performance standards reset each year?

A: Once the [State Board of Education] adopts a set of standards, the state carries that expected level of performance from year to year. Each year, a new edition of the test is developed. Most of the questions on the test are new, but some have appeared in previous years. The repeated items are called "anchor" items. They are used to link the performance on one year's edition of a state test to earlier editions. This procedure is called "equating." Equating the current year's state test to state tests given in previous years makes comparing yearly results fairer.[4]

Standardized tests change almost constantly, though. From 2009 to 2011, some schools in this same state took a different test for three successive years. For several years up to and including 2009, the annual assessment was a six-day test, over two weeks. In eighth grade that was two days of tests for math, two for science, and two for reading. Each grade had a bit different configuration: seventh grade, for instance, did two math, two reading, and two writing. All tests were on paper, written with pencils.

In 2010, a newly elected state superintendent renamed and redesigned the test, though it was unclear exactly what that meant at the time, since only state insiders had access to the redesign process. The same year, some schools took part or all of the test online, instead of on paper. The third year (2011), the test was cut down to three days (one for each subject tested), and some schools returned to paper/pencil, while others remained online, while still others started online for the first time. (Online testing involved a significant "training" aspect for students, as the online test had numerous features—the ability to highlight passages, for instance—designed to replicate what students could have done with pencil on paper. Suffice to say, the state education bureaucracy was very concerned to be sure that students knew how to use the online testing platform.)

If discussions of validity and comparability were had, they were not particularly public, so educators and parents were left in a "trust us" situation—this with tests that should really more accurately be called the "still standardizing" tests, or the "in transition to new formats, but not changing the standardization of content—as far as you know" tests.

Then in 2012, the state superintendent announced yet another plan to change the test. With the legislature having made the money available for it, he announced his desire to explore the usefulness of so-called formative tests, done at the beginning of the learning, with more and smaller tests through the year. Not only would this help teachers help students by providing a baseline against which to show a student his/her growth, it would help determine teacher impact on student growth more accurately and usefully.

In theory, joining the Common Core State Standards consortium, which all but a few states have done, will mitigate the problems with variability in the test. The consortium generates a set of tests that follow from the standards, and all participants will then be able to take the same tests. Consistency over time, however, is far from guaranteed, as the same practical and philosophical concerns will attend the consortium's annual tests as do each state's individual tests. To presume otherwise is either hubris or naïveté.

Teachers whose performance will be based on student growth would likely be interested in such a consistent arrangement, but the point here is that the standardized tests may not be quite as standard as we would hope. Even so, perhaps student performance can improve by incentivizing teachers and students to do better work. Here, too, we get more confusion than clarity, because the tests surely create incentives . . . it's just not clear for what and for whom.

If you've spent more than a few minutes around a conversation about schools and testing, you've likely heard the phrase *high-stakes testing*. Most mentions of this topic, though, are invocations of a shibboleth, usually about how wrong-minded or badly constructed the tests are. The public discussion of high-stakes testing deals precious little, though, with the issue of who is being incentivized to do what.

The test outcomes have almost no impact on the students and their academic lives, so neither the stakes nor the incentives are high for them. Rather, teachers feel the pressure of the high stakes, and increasingly so when student performance on those tests is going to be a factor in teacher evaluations, as it will undoubtedly be almost everywhere soon.

But any notion that we can rightly and wisely connect student scores to teacher evaluations suffers from several serious logical errors or flaws. Here we must take a brief walk through the woods of logic. First, and most importantly, using the test scores to demonstrate teacher quality is a claim badly constructed. In the language of scientific method, such a claim relies on affirming the consequent, an act ruled invalid in the logic of enquiry and analysis.

The purported cause (Teacher Impact) is observed as the effect on the presumed outcome (Test Score). In other words, Teachers —> Test Score changes. Seems clear enough: bad teacher will generate lower test scores; good teacher will generate good test scores. But we are measuring both cause (Teacher Impact) and effect (Test Score)—with the same data, namely, Test Score.

To construct the causal sequence in this fashion makes the claim tautological. Good scores equal good teacher and bad scores bad teacher . . . the scores prove it. In other words, Test Scores serve as the operational measure of both the student and the teacher—one piece of data measures both the independent and dependent variables.

To make this a plausibly valid claim we must define measures of Teacher Impact—or "Good" Teacher—prior to and separate from Test Scores, then hypothesize that higher/better Teacher Impact ratings will cause higher Test Scores. Unfortunately, this is not how the analysis proceeds, because it's far too easy to simply define teacher quality by Test Score results.

The second problem with connecting scores and evaluations is more sociological. Such connections implicitly look upon the students as neutral actors in the whole scenario. In doing so, we assume students are merely objects being turned or maneuvered by teachers and that whatever teachers do well or badly transmits fairly directly to students and shows up in their test scores. If student scores go up, that teacher did a good job. If not, not.

Let's suppose, instead, that we want to measure Teacher Impact on something called Student Performance, which is constituted in part (or in whole) by a measurement called Test Score. If something intervenes between the cause (Teacher Impact) and the outcome (Student Performance) which causes the measurement device (Test Score) to register something more or less than actual Teacher Impact on Student Performance, then Test Score is a less than fully accurate accounting of Teacher Impact.

In other words, for the test to be a useful measure of a teacher's influence on a student's achievement we have to assume that Student Performance measured as Test Scores is actually an accurate (if logically invalid) measure of Teacher Impact. Such assumptions are dubious, at best, as much intervenes between Teacher and Test Score.

Even if we could solve all these logical problems, we would still have a third concern—motivation. Students—for whom the tests have no apparent relevance—take the tests, and their scores are a measure of accountability for the teacher, not for the student. You don't even have to have read *Nudge* or an economics text to ponder the obvious disconnect between incentive and behavior.

To put it in perhaps too much of a social science kind of way, the agents (students) whose practical ability we are hoping to see (registered as test score outcomes) don't have adequate incentives to maximize performance. Nor does the school or teacher possess some sort of authority that could compel students to seek maximal outcomes over and against their own preferences to do so. Instead, teachers are to induce good performance from students. Every teacher knows, of course, that some students will simply not be so induced.[5]

The tests may not motivate students, but they surely motivate teachers. Keeping your job, after all, is a significant incentive, so no one should be surprised to think that teachers would incline their work in the direction of maximizing test scores. Cheating is but the furthest response to that incentive. There is little need to discuss here the scandalous cases of inappropriate conduct by teachers and administrators in various districts around the United States. The incentives in such cases are clear enough.

Another more nuanced and interesting aspect of these cheating cases does bear consideration, though. One of the methods used to identify systemic cheating is based on the statistical analysis of student performance on tests.[6] Student performance grows at predictable rates, so score changes outside the predicted domain are deemed suspect and warranting investigation.

Education reformers and scholars seem to take little note of the fact that human beings have a somewhat predictable growth trajectory, even academically. Instead, we are busily constructing a culture in which a superstar teacher is supposed to bring students along faster than the normal rate, but only within a reasonable parameter or else it will raise the specter of cheating.

If job security remains too abstract, perhaps money—for both students and teachers—can motivate more effectively. Recent studies confirm what some parents have already tried with their own children—payoffs for good grades. Rewards boost performance by increasing motivation, especially if the reward is promised right before the test and granted right after the test. The review of one University of Chicago study puts it drolly, "The rewards apparently provide students with an incentive to take tests more seriously."[7] No one has yet seriously suggested system-wide policies of paying students for good results. The few cases where a local educator or administrator has tried this have been freighted with discord.

Monetary incentives can also work for teachers. Another University of Chicago study found students achieved as much as a 10 percentile increase in their scores compared to students with similar backgrounds, if their teacher received a bonus at the beginning of the year (with the condition that teachers would have to return the bonus for unmet student growth targets). There was no gain for students when teachers were offered the bonus at the end of the school year.[8]

This sounds promising, but think about the nudge (well, shove, perhaps) hereby constructed. Given the specific growth areas to be targeted, and with the threat of money to be taken away, we can easily imagine that those teachers would make certain they pushed hard in the target areas. The authors rightly claim that they have demonstrated the power of loss aversion to motivate people.

They did not prove, however, that students got a "good education" from such a teacher reward scheme, insofar as we are left to assume that the 10 percent growth was in areas that are in fact important, and were not achieved at the expense of educational areas not identified as growth targets for the bonus.

Another difficulty with monetized incentive schemes arises more generally in the rush to create innovative programs. Innovation gets financial and political support, without necessarily proving that it works. A review of federal innovation programs observed that the programs were to start "awarding bigger grants in return for greater evidence of program effectiveness. . . . The idea is to encourage developers to scale up proven programs and strategies while at the same time seeding research on less-tested ideas."[9]

Certainly, this incentivizes the managers of those grant-receiving programs to maximize their results (and thereby maintain ongoing grant revenues), and likely raises the prospect that outcome data will be managed in such a way as to show better results. Loss aversion, after all, is the strongest motivator.

More generally, every institutional arrangement (in this case, the program development that is stimulated by grant money availability) creates both opportunity and constraint, as well as both intended and unintended consequences. It shouldn't take a PhD in organizational leadership to know that if we incentivize people with the promise of big grant money for big results, they will try to create programs that show big results.

Moreover, unless we are completely sure that the big results on the particular program measures correlate well with what we really want to accomplish in the education process, some of those programs created in response to the grant money incentive will simply be for the sake of showing results in order to get the money.

The logic of loss aversion applies to organizations as well as it does to individuals, after all. The grant recipients don't have to be consciously or intentionally instrumental in seeing their program's results only in terms of maintaining funding. Instead, such a reward/incentive system creates a culture and climate that subtly encourages people to focus on program results (some form of test score) so emphatically as to make them a kind of shibboleth, and by which they neglect other values possibly worth maintaining and pursuing.

Clearly, the direct intention of the high payoff for high performance is to stimulate achievement of students in school. But every institutional arrangement generates more than we intend. When those who are being so incentivized figure out just what measures of "high performance" are going to be rewarded, they will target their programs at that. And in the nature of the case they will target other things less emphatically.

We are assuming, in other words, that the grant money for performance actually translates down to outcomes that we actually want in students. Since students are not a monolithic group with monolithic goals, hopes, aspirations, and needs, we should understand that no institutional arrangement will meet every goal we value. This has been true since the first organizational relationship was entered into. Dangling even more money in front of people will not solve this fundamental organizational problem.

A final concern about the standardized test process involves the scoring and analysis. While there is plenty to say about the mechanics of the scoring process, a bit of which we will consider in the next chapter, determining which scores to use and what they mean are even more serious and, of course, complicated. Consider the different school assessments below. Each one is derived from the same test results in one school.

The first chart lists the pass rates on the reading exams for this particular school, from 2008 to 2012. Note that students take each of the state exams near the end of the school year, but the results are not available until approximately October.

If you are an "outsider" to this discussion, you are probably wondering what in the world to do with these numbers. What, for instance, do they show about how "good" this school—or at least its reading/language arts program—is? What, if anything, do these numbers do to help students? Good questions, both. The answers, unfortunately, aren't so clear.

As we will see shortly, these numbers are pretty respectable. Of course, even in hearing that, you might wonder, "compared to what?" Herein lies the problem. The education establishment tends to make odd comparisons with the numbers, rendering all this data less useful than it might be.

For instance, teachers talk informally amongst themselves about how a group does through the years. If you move one number to the right and one number down, you are tracking the score for the same cohort of students as it moves up the years. The 2008 sixth graders passed at 84.9 percent. As

Reading Pass Rates	2008	2009	2010	2011	2012
6th Grade	84.9	79.7	66.1	84.2	77.8
7th Grade	73.2	74.2	69.2	70.4	79.5
8th Grade	72.1	80.3	82.8	78.6	76

seventh graders in 2009 they passed at 74.2 percent. The previous spring's score is the closest thing to a baseline that this year's teacher has available, so tracking one's current students' previous scores gives a teacher some general sense of what got accomplished during that year.

This is a rough and somewhat variable measurement device, especially in districts with high rates of transience. But it is about the best a teacher or staff can do with the official data. This is not what the insiders—the state education bureaucrats—do with the data, though. Typically, they look at a teaching cohort, not a student cohort. In other words, they compare eighth-grade performance, for example, across the years. After all, if we are moving all students to proficiency against the standards, we should see each grade level—indeed, each teacher—show improved performance over prior years, irrespective of the change in students from year to year.

The school represented by the scores above, for instance, earned a School of Distinction award (twice in consecutive years) . . . for improved seventh-grade scores, year on year. The school was one of few to win consecutive year awards, unsurprisingly, for improvements in the same grade level year after year have a natural ceiling. Moreover, no one has yet pointed out that if you want to win distinction awards, there is some advantage to starting out with low success rates, the more room in which you then have to show improvement.

Another question an outsider might have is, why are seventh-grade reading scores so often lower than eighth and sixth? The seventh graders take both reading and writing exams, and the same class/teacher takes primary leadership in teaching both. While writing is important for sixth- and eighth-grade students and teachers, there is no writing test that year. But seventh-grade English or language arts teachers get the same number of instructional minutes to prepare for both reading and writing tests as sixth- and eighth-grade teachers get to prepare for a reading test only.

The seventh-grade teachers in this particular school made a choice to work hard to improve student writing. In a span of a few years, writing pass rates went from the mid-60s to the mid-80s. Happily, the seventh-grade reading scores are strong, too, but with the same amount of instructional time for two tests, seventh-grade language arts teachers in Washington state face a different array of opportunity costs than do sixth- and eighth-grade language arts teachers.

We have thus far considered the simple pass/fail distinction in the test scores, and, indeed, these are the numbers the state highlights and the media report. The state does report, however, a further breakdown in these basic scores, using four levels instead of two. Level 3 and 4 are both passing; level 3 means meeting standard, with a score of 400–418 in reading, 400–436 in math, and 400–430 in science.

Level 4 means exceeding standard, with a reading score of 419 or higher, math score of 437 or higher, and science score of 431 or higher. (There's confusion, if not complexity.) Level 2 and 1 breakdowns are the same across the tests. Level 2 means below standard, with a score of 376–399 and level 1 means well below standard with a score of 375 or lower.

The second table reports the eighth-grade reading results—percentage passing—for the same school, 2009–2012. (The results in the parentheses are for all of Washington state, offered here as another basic metric of comparison.) Adding the further—even if minor—distinction shown here generates a potentially far richer, and more complicated, picture.

First, the overall pass rate for the eighth grade at this particular school shows both steadiness and superiority over the state average. This would be pleasing to the teachers, administrators, and school leadership. Level 4 performance—exceeds standard—has grown and is also substantially above the state average.

Essentially all of the movement—from one level to another—has been from level 3 to level 4, and both of the "not passing" levels have remained basically constant. (State performance has changed in almost precisely the same degree.) Under the current reporting system, such movement is irrelevant. Moving from level 2 (not passing) to level 3 (passing) would change the overall pass rate, which is the goal. Any other movement does not register on the school's results.

Having added the extra levels to the pass/fail scoring also enables us to create a different scoring metric, and this is precisely what one education policy interest group has done. The Fraser Institute created an average based on the aggregation of the scores for all four test levels. The third table shows these scores. (Their reportage covered only 2006–2009.)

The OSPI (Washington state's Office of the Superintendent of Public Instruction) Report Card shows the percentage of eighth graders (from the same school described above) who passed the reading test. The number in parentheses indicates the seventh grade (previous year) pass rate for the same group. The EFF-Fraser score is determined by simply averaging all the test scores according to the four-level breakdown.

8th grade reading	2009	2010	2011	2012
Overall at Standard	79.6 (67.5)	82.8 (69.4)	78.6 (68.7)	76 (67.3)
Level 4	48.4 (34.3)	51.2 (43.1)	56.7 (44.2)	56.4 (42.5)
Level 3	31.3 (32.5)	31.5 (25.6)	21.8 (23.8)	19.6 (24.1)
Level 2	14.2 (21.1)	13.3 (18.8)	14.7 (19.1)	14.4 (19.0)
Level 1	5.3 (9.8)	3.4 (10.7)	5.9 (11.1)	5.6 (12.2)

	2006	2007	2008	2009
OSPI Report Card	70.1% passing	74.2% (65.9)	72.1% (74.6)	79.6% (73.2)
EFF-Fraser	3.1	3.05	3.01	3.25

Again, the state education bureaucracy only measures the proportion of "passes"—3s and 4s, though without distinguishing them—out of all tests taken. The EFF-Fraser reporting adds up all scores and divides by the number of tests taken. A couple of things are interesting here. As we have already noted, the state scoring system takes no account of a student moving from 1 to 2, or 3 to 4, or the other direction. Moving above or below 400 is all that affects the "score" (percentage). In the Fraser scoring system, movements from 1 to 2 and 3 to 4 (or reverse) do affect the overall average.

Another interesting feature is that while the percentage of this school's eighth graders passing in 2007 was greater than 2006, the Fraser average went down. This must mean that the 2007 students achieved more 3s and fewer 4s (or more 1s and fewer 2s) than the 2006 eighth graders, who had a lower OSPI pass rate, but a higher Fraser average. Finally, Fraser uses the trend in a school's scores to assign a trajectory status to the school. This school was determined to be trending up, apparently based on the change from 2008 to 2009.

So, which metric should we use to evaluate a school or a teacher? These few data points indicate that the two scoring systems don't necessarily correlate. Further, the Fraser average is a blunt instrument. Since a student earning a 400 and another earning a 418 both get 3s, we cast into the same category what are really quite different outcomes. But the percentage passing calculation (OSPI) is even more blunt. For example, 375 is the cutoff between a 1 and 2. For the OSPI calculation, this difference means nothing. For the Fraser calculation, it means a lot.

Think about teacher incentives under the two different scoring systems. If teachers were rated on the Fraser system, getting a student from 374 to 376 would matter because a 1 moving to a 2 would help the overall rating. Under the OSPI scoring system, a teacher would have much less interest in such a change, as it would have no impact on pass rates.

This is no mere academic discussion, though. In practical terms, 26 points is a lot to hope a student at 374 will gain on the current year's exam. The different scoring systems, then, can affect the amount of "attention" and support such a student will get. Under the OSPI system, when test season approaches, the bubble students (390 and up) will get the extra support opportunities more than the 374s. Under the Fraser scoring, a teacher/school would have as much incentive to support 374s as 399s.

Of course, neither scoring system takes account of a student's movement from 376 to 399, or 400 to 418, or 419 to 450 and beyond. But if changes in score reflect student growth, each of these is significant . . . much more significant than 399 to 400. No scoring system will be as sharp as we might like, but we can certainly do better than the two-level pass/fail structure we currently use.

The variation in ways to look at scores also has serious implications for the issue of evaluating teachers. Value-added models (VAMs)[10] of teacher evaluation are touted, by some, as a great instrument for assessing teachers and how they contribute to growth in student performance. Michelle Rhee instituted such a program in Washington, DC, during her tenure as chancellor of schools there. Plenty of other school districts and interest groups are now pushing to adopt some sort of VAM.

There are many benefits to such models. Indeed, some school districts already use the more frequent assessments so essential to the VAM, testing students in September, January, and May. From this, teachers can look at beginning-of-year performance and compare it to end-of-year in order to see how much students "grew" during that year in a particular subject area.

Proponents of such testing as part of the teacher evaluation process assure us they can isolate the teacher's contribution to student growth (as opposed to other factors beyond school), and maybe they can. What isn't clear is just how we ought to compile the scores. Will a teacher's class average growth determine the value added, or will the raw number of gainers and decliners be tallied, irrespective of the quantities of movement in either direction? Or something else?

More importantly, nobody seems to have asked how this affects high-achieving schools and their teachers. The VAM guidelines cited above suggest that teachers who generate higher than expected growth be assessed higher than those who generate expected or below expected growth. That makes sense. The problem is the growth expectation patterns are based upon where you are initially. If a student starts in the ninety-eighth percentile, expected growth will be very small, especially compared to a student in the twenty-fifth percentile.

Ostensibly, this difference is corrected when you say "achieves higher than expected" growth. But every teacher knows that really good and capable students (say, those in the percentile ranks above ninety) often "wobble"— successive test scores bounce around a high mark, but one test to the next may not show improvement. It remains unclear whether to count such wobbling as "less than expected performance" when a student tests at ninety-eighth percentile in fall and "slips" to ninety-sixth in spring. That student is operating at a very high level, and those few points' drop would consist of a substantial element of predictable statistical variation.

On the other hand, students who start low have a lot of room for rapid growth. Of course, the expected growth is higher, and so is the risk that the student might remain disengaged from schooling and the testing, and thereby show (much) lower than expected growth. The point is that a different set of prospects (and risks) attend the VAM programs in the different settings.

In the school depicted by the numbers above, the eighth graders typically come in reading—as a group—somewhere in the ninth grade level, maybe early tenth grade. Typically, they are sent on to ninth grade a little bit more than a year ahead of where they came in. But what would happen if students achieved only eight months' equivalent of growth in the nine months in school? Would that be deemed "less than expected"? Probably so, even though 8/9ths of expected growth, when they're already nearly two years ahead, may be normal wobble.

There's one last quirk about teacher incentives under a VAM. With a fall test baseline and a spring test assessment of the year's growth, teachers will want students to come in lower than their actual ability on their fall test. In that way, a lot of "easier" growth can be achieved for spring. To put it most coarsely, teachers would be okay with students—especially high-performing students—having significant summer drop-off, so that the fall test shows an aberrantly low outcome.

By March of every school year, you can be sure that practically every school in the United States begins an earnest "gearing up" process for the upcoming state test. You might call it the "testing season." Teachers review test-like questions, talk about test structure and strategies, give out practice exams (released from their state's testing bureaucracy), and, perhaps, offer "extended learning opportunities" (after-school classes) for so-called bubble kids. The fondest hope of administrators and teachers is to get a few of last year's "almost passed" students to passing this year (and keep passers from slipping below the bar). That would make the relevant school numbers go up.

Faced with opportunity costs, though, there are things not being done, at the same time. The students who are safely in the passing zone, who could probably forego even the test prep done as part of the regular general education day, are left doing less than they probably could do. During test season, this matters little, though. Since teachers are not really held accountable for changes in student scores, only whether they pass or not, we should not expect them to do those things they have little incentive to do.

Take, as an example, an English teacher. The more students who pass the reading test, the better. It doesn't really matter whether those students grow in their enjoyment of reading, or do more of it. If teaching test strategies makes those numbers go up, great . . . the better pass rate will make that teacher a hero.

So, the question still remains, what does passing the standardized test prove other than the fact that you passed the standardized test? If a teacher can get marginal readers or mathematicians or scientists or writers up over the magic bar, does that mean they're now better students, will be more successful in their pursuits, are smarter than before they passed? Maybe if the tests are good enough, we could answer yes to these questions. We turn next, then, to the task of assessing the assessment.

NOTES

1. Neil Postman, "Language Education in a Knowledge Context," *Et cetera*, Spring (1980): 25-37, http://neilpostman.org/articles/etc_37-1-postman.pdf.

2. Richard Thaler and Cass Sunstein, *Nudge: Improving Decisions About Health, Wealth, and Happiness* (New Haven, CT: Yale University Press, 2008).

3. See the Common Core explanation of these at "English Language Arts Standards » Reading: Informational Text » Grade 8," *Common Core State Standards Initiative* (blog), http://www.corestandards.org/ELA-Literacy/RI/8.

4. Office of the Superintendent of Public Instruction, "Frequently Asked Questions About State Testing." http://www.k12.wa.us/assessment/statetesting/faq.aspx.

5. For an overview of the organizational requirements of establishing environments that encourage compliant behavior, see Ronald Mitchell, "Regime Design Matters: Intentional oil pollution and treaty compliance," *International Organization*, 48, no. 3 (1194): 425-58, http://rmitchell.uoregon.edu/sites/default/files/resume/articles_refereed/1994-IO.pdf. Mitchell explains what he calls the strategic triangle of compliance—incentives to act, ability to monitor, and capacity to enforce, which must be appropriately arrayed with the individuals who have the wherewithal to execute each function. In the case of education, this is student performance measured as test score maximization, and the triangle does not get rightly made. The actors with incentives (Teachers) have some, but limited, impact on the actors with the practical capacity (Students) to maximize scores, and the actor with "legal" authority (Parents) to compel the exercise of greater student capacity has been dropped out of the scenario.

6. Sean Mulvenon, Ronna Turner, and Shawn Thomas, *Techniques for Detection of Cheating on Standardized Tests using SAS®* (Working paper, University of Arkansas, Fayetteville), http://www2.sas.com/proceedings/sugi26/p257-26.pdf; and Brian Jacob and Stephen Levitt, "Rotten Apples: An Investigation Of The Prevalence And Predictors Of Teacher Cheating," *Quarterly Journal of Economics*, 118, no. 3 (2003): 843-78, http://sitemaker.umich.edu/bajacob/files/cheating.pdf.

7. Rick Nauert, "Immediate Reward Hikes Student Performance," *Psych Central*, June 27, 2012. http://psychcentral.com/news/2012/06/27/immediate-reward-hikes-student-performance/40735.html.

8. William Harris, "Student performance improves when teachers given incentives up front." See more are http://news.uchicago.edu/article/2012/08/08/student-performance-improves-when-teachers-given-incentives-upfront.

9. Sarah Sparks, "Innovation Criteria Is a Model for Feds," *Education Week*, October 26, 2011. http://www.edweek.org/ew/articles/2011/10/26/10innovation.h31.html.

10. Justin Baer, Michaela Gulemetova, and Cynthia Prince, "Research Guidance to State Affiliates on Value-Added Teacher Evaluation Systems" (Working paper, National Education Association), http://vibrantschoolstacoma.org/wp-content/uploads/2011/07/NEA-VAM-best-practices-guide.pdf.

Chapter Six

Standardized Tests and the Complexity of Learning

[T]exts, like those on reading tests, are filled with gaps—presumed domain knowledge—that the writer assumes the reader knows. . . . Researchers have consistently demonstrated that in order to understand what you're reading, you need to know something about the subject matter.

—E. D. Hirsch, Jr. [1]

Beyond the typical critiques of standardized testing, in this chapter we uncover the weakness of the standardized test design. An experiment done with eighth graders, in which they are taught how to decode the questions and answers without even reading the passage, and in which they scored far above expected on a no-passage, questions-only test, shows the degree to which the reading test is more a test of testing than reading. Moreover, other important tests, like the NAEP's national civics test, show similar weaknesses.

Hirsch and Pondiscio argue there's no such thing as a reading test because reading mechanics and comprehension are quite different things—think of the phonically capable Johnny who doesn't understand what he reads. This creates a disconnect between real comprehension and comprehension for the test, and allows a table-turning of the reading assessment. You can, in effect, decode the reading test.

For the past two years, some teachers have done just that for their students, teaching them how to improve comprehension for the test by reviewing the form and structure of questions and answers on the standardized test—just the questions and answers . . . without the reading passages. After identifying the patterns in the questions and answers, the students take an eight-question reading test, without ever reading the associated passages. Later, we will see how well they did, but first the procedure.

The following tutorial is based on a three-question Office of the Superintendent of Public Instruction (OSPI—Washington state's education agency) "released item." Released items are test material available at the OSPI web site, and consist of a passage and question set that was earlier beta-tested on real students, unbeknownst to them, as a non-scored section of a real MSP (Measurement of Student Progress) test. These practice questions are intended to help students prepare for the exam. They will, instead, prepare you to "take the MSP." Following the tutorial are two sets of four questions and answers from other released items. (Correct answers follow later.)

By eighth grade, most students have up to five years of experience with state standardized tests and when reviewing these patterns, many students realized they had a general, if somewhat unconscious, awareness that they knew or at least recognized them. All patterns explained here have been identified by several years of working with OSPI released items, and listening to students observe—in ways only teenagers can—the similarity between released items and actual test items. Teachers are forbidden—along with everyone besides students and the state bureaucrats—from looking at actual MSP tests.

Clearly, released items are not test items, but with a review process as tortuous as what each item must pass through, released items and actual test items are unlikely to be significantly different. Indeed, the bias and sensitivity screening that prospective test items go through narrows the range of acceptable material, and helps to make this pattern discernment possible. Moreover, if released and actual items varied too widely, then released items would be of little value to students, and the students' years of experience with real test questions wouldn't transfer to success on this test based on released items.

Here, then, is the primer on how to take the standardized test (in Washington state, at least), starting with question and answer samples, then explanations of the patterns in view.

1. What is the main idea of "Excerpt from Iditarod Dream"?

    a. Sled dog racing is a thrilling and dangerous sport.
    b. Sled dog racing requires teamwork and training.
    c. Sled dog racing requires specialized equipment.
    d. Sled dog racing can be a family activity.

First, this is a main idea question, so the answer needs to be "worthy" of serving as a main idea. It's hard to explain, but ask a nearby eighth grader, and he or she will understand that some of these just don't "feel" like test-type main idea answers. They're not serious or important or high-quality enough, or at least they're not as serious as some other options.

"Specialized equipment" isn't as important a point as either "teamwork and training" or "thrilling and dangerous." "Family activity" is almost non-sensical in that it violates expectation of what we might think or hear about dog sledding. While there may indeed be a family out there that makes sledding one of its activities, this would be an oddity. This test doesn't usually make main points out of oddities.

"Teamwork and training" or "thrilling and dangerous" are the best options, then. But this state test often includes readings with a kind of moral element. There are an unusual number of uplifting or inspiring stories. Whether a little-known figure gallant for service to others, or a determined soul who has surmounted obstacles to achieve something and/or (better yet) learned some important life lesson, test questions go through a vetting process that renders controversial or negative material unlikely to make the final cut.

Thinking of it in this way, "thrilling and dangerous" has just a hint of the selfish and irresponsible. "Teamwork and training," by contrast, is the kind of emphasis the test can and likes to support. If you were inclined to go with that, you would be right.

2. According to "Excerpt from Iditarod Dream," why does Dusty decide to help the other racers build a fire?

   a. He uses the fire light to see the trail markers.
   b. He thinks the fire will help him stay awake.
   c. He is following the rule of the wilderness.
   d. He needs to cook the dogs' frozen meat.

Sometimes, test answers can tend toward the "odd one out" option, especially if it is separated from the others by its depth, breadth, or importance. C jumps out immediately because it's of a different quality from the others, which are all specific and concrete things. C, by contrast, is an interestingly oblique answer that hints of something "higher" than the other three. The combination of uniqueness and grandness makes C too hard to pass up, and doing so would yield a wrong answer—C is correct.

3. According to "Excerpt from Iditarod Dream," how would Dusty most likely react to entering another dog sled race?

   a. He would be hopeful because he came so close to winning.
   b. He would be nervous because he had trouble staying on the trail at night.

c. He would be excited because he knew how it felt to cross the finish line in the lead.

d. He would be anxious because he ran out of supplies and needed more for the next race.

On first blush, this ostensibly "prediction" question seems unanswerable without reading the passage. Indeed, how can we predict anything with such a dearth of knowledge of the situation. Further, each answer option contains a detail that we can only guess at, so we're left with a higher degree of uncertainty than in the previous questions. But ultimately we are trying to get the correct test answer here, not predict something about Dusty, so things are not as hopeless as they seem.

First, cover all the answers from the word "because" onward. You are left with a list of adjectives about how Dusty would feel. The traditional advice to "look for the stronger word," and the current advice to think about uplift and inspiration could be of some help. Granted, every test item won't work this way, but following these two "rules," C—excited—breaks out to an early lead in the race to pick the correct answer. Option A has the tinge of the overly competitive.

Test answers probably tend to de-emphasize things like winning. Just look how the test renders "winning" in option C—"knew how it felt to cross the finish line in the lead." The test authors seem at pains to avoid a word that sits uncomfortably in the social culture of collaborative education. Many eighth graders may not follow or care about the culture of education, but they do pick up on patterns, and the combination of that quirky way of saying "win" and the most upbeat adjective—"excited"—make C a plausible option.

Granted, this explanation is much more abstruse and convoluted, so take another approach by covering every answer from the adjective back to the beginning of the sentence and leave exposed what really are the first part of four conditional statements. For instance, option A can rearrange to say "He came close to winning, so he will be hopeful."

Note that not all the events can occur in the story. How could Dusty come close to winning and cross the finish line in the lead? He can't, so either A or C is incorrect. It's unlikely that both A and C are incorrect, as Dusty had to either win or not win, and the answer set would be strangely perplexing if one of the causal elements (latter part of the statement) were true but that answer were wrong. It would indeed be a more challenging test if readers had to actually make inferences about Dusty's feeling—by, say, dealing with several true statements. But such are not as easily graded as a standardized test needs to be.

Turning to the "deep" or "serious" test, D is the least likely—it does not have the feel of high level of thinking. B is a contender, but its chances are reduced by the difficulty of both A and C then being incorrect. So, if it must be A or C, the odd wording for "win" in C is too strong a pull to avoid. (This unusual wording, which distracts some testers, is another issue entirely. Some students will be vexed by the difference between "win" and "cross the finish line in the lead," and so will not be sure if this is the right answer. This vexation will help ensure that some students will get the answer wrong, thereby creating the necessary distribution of answers and scores. This opens a whole different problem—the effort to measure whether individual students are meeting a standard by misusing testing devices and procedures whose design actually distributes students across the outcome spectrum.)

Now, when finally reading the passage, all a tester really has to do is simply confirm which of the events described in the latter part of each sentence actually happened. Did Dusty win? If so, it's C. Most of the time the option set will contain only one accurate description of an event which actually occurs in the story, making the corresponding answer option the obvious choice.

The student taking the test does not really have to predict, he/she just has to look for which of the events described in the answer options really did happen. Almost certainly only one occurred, but in the effort to make the test something more than matching (the story event to the correlated answer option) some slightly inaccurate permutation of one of the other events will appear as an answer. In this case, the oddly inaccurate one is the "going off the trail" option (B), and the correct answer is indeed C.

Interestingly, this question was categorized as "comprehension," which presumably ranks below "analysis" (which "prediction" would be) on the intellectual spectrum. The question is framed to look like a prediction question but really isn't. The student's ability to comprehend which detail (from the latter half of each answer option) actually happened in the story is really what's getting tested. Students needn't predict anything. This question was the hardest to answer without reading the passage, but many testers were able to narrow it down to two answers and C was usually one of them.

With these now finely honed test decoding skills, take some multiple choice test questions.

Story 1—Nurses in the Wilderness

1. Which sentence tells how the Frontier Nursing Service and the Mary Breckinridge Hospital are similar?

   a. Both have modern supplies.
   b. Both provide rural medical services.
   c. Both are located in Wendover, Kentucky.
   d. Both train people from all over the world.

2. What is most likely the author's main purpose for writing this selection?

    a. To inform the reader about the history of rural nursing
    b. To describe the effects of diseases on rural children
    c. To persuade the reader to support rural medicine
    d. To explain the difficulty of travel in rural areas

3. According to the captions in the selection, which statement is true?

    a. Nurses often called Mary an angel on horseback.
    b. Patients were sometimes carried to clinics by neighbors.
    c. Mary's first clinic became the Mary Breckinridge Hospital.
    d. Riding horseback was the only form of travel to the hospital.

4. Which sentence best summarizes the selection?

    a. Mary and her family were always very generous to others.
    b. The Frontier Nursing Service reached far beyond Kentucky.
    c. Rural nurses found creative ways to transport supplies and patients.
    d. Mary and other nurses provided compassionate medical care to rural people.

Story 2 — A Touch of Genius

5. Which sentence from the selection is an opinion?

    a. "The same process happens with me."
    b. "He lost his sight and partial use of one hand."
    c. "I had no words to describe the emotion I felt."
    d. "Behind this statement lies a remarkable story."

6. Which sentence best states the main idea of the selection?

    a. Michael served in Vietnam.
    b. Michael is a talented artist.
    c. Michael teaches sculpture in the pueblo.
    d. Michael has displays in museums around the world.

7. Which statement is the most important conclusion that may be drawn from the selection?

    a. War teaches people to be strong.
    b. Art can make a difference in a child's life.

c. Hardships can motivate a person to greatness.
d. Mothers have a great influence on their children.

8. After reading this selection, what generalization can you make about Michael?

a. Michael is a motivated individual.
b. Michael is an excellent teacher.
c. Michael likes military service.
d. Michael loves animals.

With the revelation of these patterns fresh in mind, ninety-five eighth grade students took one of two different versions of an eight-question, no-reading passage test like those above. The whole test consisted of the title of the passage, followed by four questions on the passage, each question with four answer options. Presumably, each student's average score would be in the area of two corrects (one out of four), as would the overall average of all students.

Having worked with the test patterns, students predicted that scores would be significantly higher than what random chance would expect. As it turned out, the average for the 95 students was 5.1 corrects, 2.5 times the expected outcome from chance. The standard deviation of this result was 1.38. The t-test p value for these results is 0.0001. In other words, the probability that 95 testers would average 5.1 corrects when they should have averaged 2 (according to chance) is exceedingly low.

Eighty-nine of the same eighth graders repeated the procedure a week later, using eight different question and answer sets. This time the only instruction was to "think about the patterns we talked about last week." In the second round, the group average was 5.3 corrects with a standard deviation of 1.33. These results also return a p value of 0.0001. If possible, the student performance in the second test was even more "extremely statistically significant" than in the first test. The following year, approximately one hundred students repeated the same process, and achieved similar results.

The replication of this test of students' ability to identify patterns in questions and answers calls into doubt the accuracy and usefulness of (at least) Washington state's standardized reading multiple choice questions. The findings raise a variety of questions about multiple-choice test items, and none of the likely answers are good. Fundamentally, is this as good a reading test as we hope and want it to be? Or is it less a reading test than a test on test taking?

If students can identify patterns of questions and their answers and get much better-than-expected scores just from knowing and seeing those patterns, then this particular standardized test is not really testing reading ability. We could certainly claim that savvy (i.e., "smart") students will more likely figure out the patterns and get the advantage on the test, and that such savvy is positively correlated with reading ability, but this adds another layer of uncertainty into the assessment process.

Given all this—the substantially better than expected student scores, a test-writing process that probably generates a narrow range of question/answer design alternatives, the secrecy of the test production—we can only wonder at just how useful this test really is. This much is clear, though: if the test creates a choice environment, one of the choices teachers are incentivized to make involves doing everything possible to maximize scores, especially if their professional evaluation is going to be tied to the test results.

Correct Answers to No-Passage Reading Test

1. B
2. A
3. B
4. D
5. D
6. B
7. C
8. A

The multiple-choice questions are but a small part of the new brand of standardized tests, though. Tests are more nuanced these days—short answer questions make up a substantial part of a student's score. Unfortunately, these questions, and their answers, appear to have problems, too. Consider Michael, from question set 2 above. In case you missed it, Michael is an awarding-winning artist who happens to be blind.

One of the released short answer questions about Michael reads:

> Explain how Michael became an award winning artist. Include two details from the selection in your answer.

The teacher booklet goes on to explain acceptable details respondents might use in their answers:

> Text-based details may include, but are not limited to:
>
> A. His mother was a potter/he helped her fix her clay
> B. Playing with clay as a child
> C. "I knew that what I wanted to do was be an artist someday."
> D. Making small animals in hospital after blindness/Vietnam, continued to sculpt
> E. Sculptures were photographed by newspapers

F. I get a picture in my mind/make his memories come to life
G. Inspires/leads sculpture workshops
H. Sculptures can be seen in museums/public buildings/Vatican/White House
I. People collect his work

Understand, it doesn't matter which two items a test-taker lists in his/her answer. All items are equal, even those—like H, I, and maybe E and G—which don't really "explain how he became an award-winning artist." H and I seem more the consequence of his becoming an award-winning artist, not an explanation of how he became one. If H and I are acceptable, then "how he became" does not mean causality. By the list of acceptable answers, the question must really mean something more like the event sequence of his rising to "award-winning artist status."

Perhaps this passage and associated questions were rejected for the weakness we are here exploiting or critiquing. If not, and items of this quality make it on to the test, then we really are testing our students badly.

The difficulties of testing are not confined to state standardized tests. Hirsch and Pondiscio's claim about reading tests makes sense when looking at other tests, too. This time, a recent National Assessment of Educational Progress Civics Test raises concern.[2] While those analyzing the results lament the lack of progress in eighth and twelfth graders, they should express as much disappointment about the test itself. Consider these questions from the twelfth grade exam.

The following question refers to the statement below.

The Second World War marked the most substantial change ever in the context in which United States foreign policy is made. The world that emerged after the war had fundamentally changed in economic, political, and military ways. These changes made the world a more dangerous place, and altered the demands placed on foreign policy.

The statement calls the world after the Second World War "a more dangerous place." What specific change could one cite to support this claim?

1. The rise of the European Union (EU)
2. The signing of the General Agreement on Trade and Tariffs (GATT)
3. The decline of German military power
4. The development and spread of nuclear weapons

The real difficulty here is that, depending on your conceptual and philosophical views, one could argue any of these—thus the source of the pithy observation that the social sciences are the really hard sciences.

1. One could argue, for instance, that the EU only exists because of the American security umbrella over it, and the EU's rapid rise reorganized Western Europe into a potent power faster than it would otherwise have done following such a devastating war, thereby threatening the Soviet Union, and making the world a less safe place.
2. You could also argue that the increase in free trade (GATT) actually makes collaboration among the big and dominant economies easier, thereby making the world less safe for those smaller, developing countries. Indeed, dozens of millions of Third Worlders were killed in the years after WWII, so their world *was* less safe.
3. In slightly different contexts, some have indeed argued that a country of Germany's stature needs to have military capacity commensurate with its size and importance. To withhold that from them—as the world has done since 1945—risks their anger, not unlike the 1920s, which, of course, gave rise to the 1930s . . . a very unsafe world.

The premises of the first claim are reasonably true, though the conclusion may be based on other causes. The second conclusion is clearly true, though, again, it may or may not derive from the premises offered here. The third argument, while following logically from so-called Realist thinking, has little purchase on both the practical and moral thinking of Germans and their former antagonists.

In other words, the first three arguments all have some analytical power, just as does the argument *against* number 4. Many analysts contend that the presence of nuclear weapons actually made the world more stable—the dominant powers were much more cautious with each other because of their ability to mutually destroy the other, though they were perfectly willing to undertake violence in the developing world.

So, what's the "right" answer? Clearly, the test authors are looking for number 4, but college professors (remember, we're aiming at college readiness in education—check the crank in the preface), or high school Advanced Placement teachers, are looking for a student who can sophisticatedly render and evaluate the competing claims, not just one who will provide answers the test authors want.

By contrast, other sample questions on the twelfth grade exam[3] were strangely facile.

> What is one responsibility that modern presidents have that is NOT described in the Constitution?
>
> 1. Commanding the armed forces
> 2. Proposing an annual budget to Congress
> 3. Appointing Supreme Court justices
> 4. Granting pardons

To answer this, a student must have either read the Constitution very thoroughly and remembered that budget proposing was not listed as the president's responsibility, or remembered the list of duties summarized (in a text or the teacher's discussion) and determined that budgeting was not on that list, or recall that budget proposing is a duty that has developed over time.

The relevance of knowing this remains unclear. Understanding how presidential powers develop and shift over time, and to what effect, is certainly important, but this question does not require a student to show knowledge of this, nor should we assume a correct answer indicates such knowledge.

Another question required the student to look at a facsimile of a voter registration application and find the heading "State of New Jersey County Commissioners of Registration" to answer that "registration commissioners from the county governments" are "responsible for the registration of voters in this state." This has the awkward feel of a reading test question. It requires no particular understanding of civics, after all, to answer correctly.

In short, while it may be fair to lament that twelfth graders haven't improved on the civics exam, we should be just as concerned that passing an exam with content this weak would earn a student "college ready" status in this subject matter. Few college professors are very interested in such rote functions as a student's giving back what test authors expect, even if that professor authored the test. The test may not, then, indicate college readiness as much as we hope.

Such has not always been the case, though. We know this, in part, because popular wisdom reminds us that things used to be better, because tests were harder, more serious. Consider the eighth grade exit exam from West Virginia, 1931. This test is one of those web phenomena wherein the description of some real item or event flashes around the Internet, stirring in contemporary readers the response appropriate to the moment.

In this case, we are supposed to be shocked with how hard such a test used to be. Indeed, the *Washington Post* education blogger, Valerie Strauss, invites us to "Take this 1931 8th Grade Test (You will probably flunk)."[4] It seems such a foregone conclusion that things were far better back in some bygone era (any bygone era) that we all believe it without even realizing we believe it. But were they better?

Indeed, there are many interesting and good things about the test. The breadth of subjects is wider than we test for today. The social sciences are represented by separate tests for geography, civics, and history. Spelling and penmanship get their due alongside reading and English, which is a bit of grammar. The social studies questions are wonderfully engaging open-ended questions demanding explanatory answers. "Why are the textile mills disappearing from New England?" "Explain the part played by agricultural machinery in national development."

That's all well and good. But there are also some surprisingly deficient things about the test. Take the reading exam. The test asks primarily recall questions about works the student has read (or was supposed to read). We just covered one angle on how students do not necessarily need to read on contemporary reading tests. For this 1931 test, they need to have read and now recall things like who wrote what piece or passage. This is partly a test of memory then. Further, we all know that some students can give an effective "short report" on books (one of the questions calls for this) they haven't actually read.

Or look at the arithmetic test. The highest math skills tested are fractions and percentages. Fractions and percentages are the beginning of the eighth-grade math year now. Indeed, algebra is nearly standard fare for eighth grade in 2013. Today, if fractions and percentages were as high as you have gone, you would take the math remediation class in eighth grade.

Turn next to the social studies section. "Connect the person with the thing he is responsible for." (By the way, Amundsen—the Norwegian polar explorer—is misspelled in this list.) This is not particularly deep social studies work. One can fairly imagine that a 1931 eighth-grade student could connect Woodrow Wilson to the 14 Points and Susan B. Anthony to Women's Suffrage without really knowing about those people or the thing for which "he" was responsible.

In short, they appear to have had the same problems with their tests back then that we have now. The tests weren't necessarily testing what they were supposed to test, they weren't very thorough, and they could be "gamed." Tests—1931 and 2013—just might be like that.

Finally, we get no detail about just how students fared on the exam. Did most pass? Did most fail? Was it an even split? Further, what percentage of fourteen-year-olds even took the test? Did some racial, socio-economic, or geographic groups finish eighth grade—and take the test—in different proportions?

At least one thing does look more serious . . . the stakes. We talk of high-stakes testing today, but look what's at stake on this 1931 test. "These [test] grades do (or do not) entitle you to an Elementary Diploma which admits you to any High School in West Virginia." This short letter is addressed to "Dear Pupil." That's a high-stakes nudge for the student, and that is different.

More than forty states have joined the so-called Common Core State Standards and the associated testing consortium that allows the members to coordinate their standard-setting and assessment. This is the closest we've yet gotten to a national education standard. One consequence of this development is that we can move even more determinedly forward to connect students' standardized test scores to teacher evaluations. Along the way, though, many teeth are gnashing over the mechanics of just how to make this linkage.

But the anxiety over implementation is only part of the story. We would do well to take a serious look at the test side of the equation. Education reformers and the business community, among others, come out big for testing, with business cheering for increased accountability of teachers and schools by way of the politically elusive test-evaluation connection.

The debate about teacher evaluations and test scores proceeds along predictable lines. Test opponents are tagged as unionists only interested in keeping cushy jobs. Test supporters are thought woefully out of touch about how classrooms really function. All the while, the test itself, that thing and process on which so much of the acrimony suspends, sits rather unassumingly by. We talk little about the test or the test process, and, by implication, bear great faith in the device and its accuracy and reliability in assessing students' knowledge and capacities.

But just how much faith should we put in the test and in procedures that use the scores as evidence to determine anything beyond whether a student did well or poorly on that specific test? Can we rely on the tests to actually and accurately measure knowledge and capability in a particular subject area?

It turns out that for the reading test at least, the answers may be disquieting. The reading assessment[5] exhibits patterns which make it more an examination of "test taking" than of reading. Sampling a few test questions indicates that we can discern a set of predictable patterns in the question-making and the answer construction. These patterns give savvy test takers an advantage and at the same time make the test a less-than-useful or accurate measure of a student's reading performance, or of how well a particular teacher is doing his or her work.

NOTES

1. E.D. Hirsch, Jr., and Robert Pondiscio, "There's No Such Thing as a Reading Test," *The Core Knowledge Blog* (blog), June 16, 2010, http://blog.coreknowledge.org/2010/06/16/theres-no-such-thing-as-a-reading-test/.

2. National Assessment of Educational Progress, "The Nation's Report Card." http://nationsreportcard.gov/civics_2010/.

3. National Assessment of Educational Progress, "The Nation's Report Card—Sample Questions." http://nationsreportcard.gov/civics_2010/sample_quest.aspx.

4. Valerie Strauss, "Take this 1931 8th grade test (you will probably flunk)," *The Answer Sheet* (blog), November 23, 2010, http://voices.washingtonpost.com/answer-sheet/history/take-this-1931-8th-grade-gradu.html.

5. The analysis of the testing process in this chapter was based largely on current state tests (for Washington), but a brief preview of the new Smarter Balanced Assessment Consortium—the assessments connected to the Common Core State Standards—reading tests reveals a basic similarity with the previous Washington state test. See http://sbac.portal.airast.org/practice-test/resources/#manuals.

Chapter Seven

Technology Adds Layer of Complication

Even when the problem of the access to technology is solved so that anyone who wishes can have access to technology, there still remains a problem.
—Neil Postman [1]

Elaborate and excessive hopes are pinned on technology as a way to improve education. Technology creates both benefits and consequences, though, and adds a new kind of complexity to schools. Further, technology that stimulates the sense of education as entertainment could undermine long-term educational goals.

We have thus far seen that the social expectations of education as a "system," the bureaucratic circumstances of schools, and the pedagogical peculiarities of the assessment process shape and distort teaching and learning. Technology is increasingly offered up as something of an antidote to these problems. American social and political culture are particularly enthralled by the idea that technology can solve our problems, so why wouldn't education be as subject to the ameliorative effects of technology as anything else?

Technology alters existing patterns of social and economic life, and in so doing stimulates strong and sometimes dramatic responses, both for and against. The more dramatic claims about how technology will transform life and work—good and bad—often end up dramatically wrong, sometimes fabulously so. Bill Gates denies ever saying that "640K (of memory) ought to be enough for everyone," but in 2004 he most assuredly did say, "Two years from now, spam will be solved." In 2013, spam accounts for about 90 percent of e-mail traffic. [2]

In 1980, *The Economist* magazine joined the growing chorus singing the praises of the paperless office. Computers, everyone thought, would enable people to do everything digitally, instead of on paper. In perhaps one of the most stunning misunderstandings of unintended consequences, such predictions neglected what easy printing and "publishing" would encourage.

When typing directly on to paper, a writer will correct mistakes on the manuscript rather than throw away all the work invested on the paper. With a printer nearby, a word-processed document can easily (and cheaply) reproduce many times. The result, *The Economist* acknowledged, has been a 50 percent increase in paper consumption since the dawn of the supposedly paperless era.[3]

Similarly dramatic claims and anxieties about technology in education abound, and they've been doing so for a long time. In the 1920s, the Society for Visual Education formed to encourage wider use of the filmstrip in education. Change to the word "Internet" or "computer" for "filmstrip" in this paragraph from a 1981 book, and you could easily find it now in numerous articles and books. "Today, the filmstrip is playing an important role in classroom instruction in all types of educational situations. Filmstrips are being used in all sizes of schools, from the small rural school to the large school in urban centers."[4]

As before, the contemporary claims and anxieties about technology are probably both overdrawn. Though technology can add breadth and richness to teaching and learning, it typically generates much less benefit than the dramatic claims promise, and much less consequence than the severest detractors warn. In fact, technology, like any other package of reform, creates both positive and negative effects, probably in about roughly equal proportion.

Technology is neither a panacea nor Pandora's Box, but it does add to the complexity of running a school and of teaching. This complexity arises largely from the somewhat mindless embrace of technology's presumed benefits—in conjunction with the seemingly willful neglect of the negatives—that allows proponents to campaign for these benefits without determining the specific effects the technology has on teaching or educational outcomes.

In the most basic organizational ways, technology adds complexity to the administrative life of a school. For instance, while web-based access to things like grades can help parents track a student's performance, teachers and administrators must work with families at different levels of access, interest, and ability to use this technology. As a bureaucratic organization, the school and its staff tend to expect all parents to fully engage these kinds of administrative tools, but, of course, many parents do not.

These heightened expectations also apply to students, for whom technology is both a boon and bane. Since they can access educational materials and resources at nearly all times from nearly anywhere, teachers can increasingly expect more responsiveness and timeliness in student work. Predictably, however, students maintain varying commitment to retrieving school material and assignments from the web, so the Internet does not generate some sort of automatic improvement in student engagement.[5]

For staff, the technologies available for teaching require scheduling and maintenance. While this may seem trivial, more than one school staff has suffered conflict over things like reserving the computer lab, or differential access to technology resources. Further, as the technologies themselves get more complicated, maintenance becomes the preserve of IT specialists, who, of course, can never satisfy the immediate demands and expectations of the technology users—teachers and staff.

The complexity of the technology itself also mounts over time, as schools must make decisions about updating outmoded infrastructure. Technology changes so fast that the most cutting-edge school built five years ago already suffers from deficiencies. The complexity rises to dizzying heights when new technologies must work with older, increasingly outdated technologies. Wire your audio/video system in a format that falls out of use, for instance, and you may find your school unable to receive television.

All the technology—and the complications it generates—does not necessarily make for a better learning environment or student performance. Amanda Ripley's discussion with an American teenager going to school in Finland—the reigning world champion of education—reveals a school dreary in appearance and appointed with no high technology, but populated with effective and motivated teachers and students.[6] Clearly, technology is neither necessary nor sufficient for good education to happen.

Some technology insiders appreciate this fact, and they're high level enough that they can resist the social climate compelling more technology in schools. A *New York Times* article that seems more a piece of satire you would expect from *The Onion* describes Silicon Valley technology people who are sending their kids to a computer-free school. Alan Eagle, a Google executive and parent in the school, says, "The idea that an app on an iPad can better teach my kids to read or do arithmetic, that's ridiculous."[7] We will see, however, that many others do not think it ridiculous. Indeed, "it's the future."

We have earlier seen that some people overlook the complications and see only positive effects of technology. A psychologist who claims that "[social media] technology is all a very positive thing," discussed in chapter 4, reflects this neglect of the complexity. There are enough cases, like those briefly discussed in chapter 1 about student-to-student and teacher-to-student misconduct, that this psychologist should understand the need for some circumspection here.

Technology advocates also misconstrue what technology is really accomplishing in the learning process, too often making breathless claims about what technology can or will do. In an article on so-called digital writing, the author offers the thesis that "the nature of writing has shifted in recent years." "Digital writing," the article points out, "is writing created or read on a computer or other Internet-connected device." This kind of writing is how "innovative teachers" use technology to engage students more in writing.[8]

The article called this "re-natured" writing, which contrasts with "traditional writing formats, such as journaling, [which] are frequently used for private reflection, [while] digital writing is almost always meant for an audience." It remains unclear—in the article, and more broadly—what re-natured means, but apparently it has something to do with making sentences composed of words by typing on a computer keyboard and posting the whole thing on the Internet. That's not really a changed nature, but rather reflects that the fundamental process and purpose of writing are nearly immutable.

This new process of writing might seem strangely traditional—merely undertaken by different media—so perhaps the difference arises in the nature of the intended audience and the material structures available to writers and readers. The e-book doesn't change the nature of writing and reading. It challenges the current publishing paradigm. But perhaps if the digital delivery mechanism has a substantive impact on what written material looks like and does, then we can say the technology has transformed writing.

No doubt, digital technologies will change content and style, but the net intellectual and practical effects of this are debatable. Gutenberg's printing press allowed an astounding transformation in reading, thinking, even perhaps religion, and part of that transformation included the erosion of the oral tradition and individual memory, over which there was, no doubt, much hand wringing at the time.

Digital technologies also generate such mixed effects. The specific consequences for developing brains, though this has just begun to be studied, appear alarming. Electronic gadgets' stimulation of dopamine (the pleasure hormone) release and the biochemical effects following therefrom are among a variety of issues neuroscientists have started to study.[9]

Teachers' visceral response to technology is caution, though. A 2012 survey of teacher attitudes about technology and its educational effects revealed a pattern of concerns that technology is winning the competition for students' attention. Teachers report a general sense of declining attention span, declining analytical depth, and increasing expectation that education entertain. One teacher noted that she is "an entertainer, [having to] do a song and dance to capture their attention."[10]

When it comes to entertainment, technology's strength may also be teaching's Achilles' heel. Indeed, by stimulating something of a Wow! desire in students, technology may feed the need for entertainment, generating short-term educational benefit in tandem with long-term detriment. Here again, emphasizing student gains on standardized tests shortens the view of what a particular educational activity or curriculum needs to accomplish, and enables the neglect of possible long-term educational outcomes, at least for a classroom teacher evaluated on the meeting of that year's narrow educational targets.

For example, more than one school around the United States uses iPads as early as preschool to teach kids their letters. In a story about one such school, a teacher said the iPads "enhance instruction." The reporter noted that one student sat, "beguiled" by the technology.[11] Unfortunately, such beguiling may not be educationally desirable for at least two reasons.

First, one effect that our short-term vision of "enhancing" things like letter learning on the iPad now is that we might stimulate an expectation for even more entertainment later. The story notes that when one student spelled "bird" correctly by lining up the letters, he got the Wow! payoff of an on-screen bird spinning around in celebration. If learning one's letters earns a stimulating reward like this, what kind of celebratory response will a student want in return for writing an essay or completing a science lab experiment?

Second, if the technology helps a student make gains on that year's narrow test-based goal, but does not contribute to broader long-term educational objectives, then the technology has actually undermined education. The implicit operating assumption is that the educational gains made with the technology will indeed transfer upward to the next level of the skill or content the student needs to learn. This is a daunting assumption about education in general—even before technology entered the scene—and is rendered no less daunting by the advent of technology.

A 2013 high schooler would not have had iPad letter learning available in preschool, but even these students' entertainment demands are heightening. In an environment where schools must get the latest and greatest technologies, or risk facing accusations of dereliction, devices like the SmartBoard are becoming ubiquitous. The chalkboard-sized touch screen monitor, which displays the teacher's computer, allows for some great opportunities like showing writing edits on screen in real time.

Unfortunately, the device's pre-packaged material also offers a variety of stylish images and graphics that are little more than eye candy. Keeping kids engaged just a little bit longer, so they might pay a little bit closer attention, may be a reasonable goal, but it does further generalize the students' need and the schools' provision of "engaging" technology.

Once technology is introduced into the environment, though, the impulse pushing educators toward entertainment intensifies. A recent *EdWeek* article on digital tools in education makes the point, even if unwittingly. Speaking first about students' entertainment lives, the author notes, "In today's digital marketplace, students of all ages can create experiences tailored just for them." Later, the author notes, "[Some] educators and schools are turning to technology and different teaching and learning approaches to give students a personalized learning experience that mirrors the customized experiences they take for granted."[12]

Notice, first, the shift toward education shaped to the student, and away from education as a process that shapes a person. Second, and more to the point of this book, technology used in support of so-called adaptive learning does indeed enhance learning, but is more complicated to implement and narrow in scope than the much more typical claims about how technology supports more efficient information transfer, wider communication opportunities, and general "access" to material.

Technology that allows adaptive learning by helping identify and then working with a student's individual weaknesses and needs requires much more than high-speed access to the Internet. It requires what education has always required—another person to work, in conjunction with the technology, along with the student.

But the very idea of technology, like best practice, is something of a trope, whose misuse allows astounding misconnection of the technology to the learning process. The school district bureaucrat in charge of the Wow! letter program observed, "This is where technology is going," and noted that schools around the country already use electronic textbooks. The comparison misleads, though, as the electronic book is a new mechanism for delivering content, while learning letters is an intellectual process—two very different things.

Technology advocates bring this all back together with a seemingly ineluctable logic, though, by pointing out how this newly digital preschool, which targets children in high-poverty neighborhoods, "levels the playing field"—gets these low-income kids more of the kind of preparation that their comparatively affluent peers get.

This rhetorical sleight of hand typically wins any discussion in which it gets used, but it doesn't take much imagination to hear the next round of demands. Since these newly lettered—but less affluent— students don't have as much access to computers and the web at home, the schools must act to rectify that imbalance, to level that part of the playing field, too.

Schools, being constrained to do only what they're organizationally capable of doing, will not think about how their own contribution to students' Wow! needs will have a deleterious effect on the students who can't access such "engaging" material at home and so end up reading less, not more, at home. Instead, the schools and the school reform drivers will push for better and more technology in the school.

The Alliance for Excellent Education did precisely this, circulating a petition urging policy makers to connect 99 percent of American students to high-speed Internet within five years. To be more precise, they want this for the schools because in today's "fast-paced global economy, all students and teachers need to be connected to the world of learning that the Internet provides."[13] In June 2013, President Obama embraced this goal for the United States.

The implicit assumption underlying all this enthusiasm for technology is that the reading mechanics learned on the Wow! device will seamlessly transfer over to reading in any and all media. Numerous informal observations, though, raise doubt about such hopes. Relying on tests of student attention while working with their electronic gadgets on, and surveys of student usage of electronic gadgets, he has found that students commit to their gadgets more than their academic work.

In one survey, seventy-six eighth graders acknowledged owning a total of 247 gadgets (iPads, iPods, smart phones, laptops, game units, etc.). They further acknowledged using 181 gadgets while doing schoolwork, though not using them for schoolwork. In other words, more than two gadgets per person competed with students' school work activities. Three different sets of attention tests with the same students showed that performance on various tasks diminished the more gadgets that were added to the mix.

Increasing numbers of studies of brains at work corroborate the conclusion that electronic distraction saps performance. But don't try to convince teenagers of that—of those seventy-six eighth graders who use more than two unrelated gadgets while doing their homework, only 18 percent said that electronics definitely (4.1 percent) or probably (13.7 percent) affect their work in a negative way.[14]

Youngsters are doing more with and on their gadgets, but socializing and entertainment grip them much more than reading (even on the gadgets) or schoolwork. Yes, these electronics may "help" with certain educational tasks in the short run, but that current use also likely creates a path dependence that stimulates increased devotion to the electronics and commensurate educational difficulty later, as the entertaining uses of the gadgets crowd out the educational uses, and traditional educational material simply dissolves into practical oblivion for students.

Unfortunately, school districts find themselves unable but to start down this path. Faith in technology, plus social demand that schools—not parents, families, or communities—do everything possible to improve outcomes, times Bill Gates insisting that computers are more effective than people equals a cultural climate in which schools must get more digital technologies, or they'll be deemed irresponsible. What gets lost in the discussion is that parents being committed to and involved in their children's education is worth much more than any technology, whether Microsoft or Apple.

Perhaps as students get older, the benefits of technology—as a content delivery mechanism—will be more clearly salutary. A substantial majority of the teachers in the survey discussed above said the Internet, at least, was mostly positive, noting that students are more self-sufficient researchers. Of course, what they produce from that more self-sufficient work may not be as good as it should be. In what the review of the survey calls the "Wikipedia problem," most teachers agree that students seem content to spit back the easy answer, typically found in the first screen of results from a web search.

Another facet of the Wikipedia problem is that it widens the scope of the oldest academic sin in the world—plagiarism. A *New York Times* article tells a story that every teacher experiences more pervasively every year:

> Jack London was the subject in Daterrius Hamilton's online English 3 course. In a high school classroom packed with computers, he read a brief biography of London with single-paragraph excerpts from the author's works. But the curriculum did not require him, as it had generations of English students, to wade through a tattered copy of "Call of the Wild" or "To Build a Fire."
>
> Mr. Hamilton, who had failed English 3 in a conventional classroom and was hoping to earn credit online to graduate, was asked a question about the meaning of social Darwinism. He pasted the question into Google and read a summary of a Wikipedia entry. He copied the language, spell-checked it and e-mailed it to his teacher.
>
> Mr. Hamilton, 18, is among the expanding ranks of students in kindergarten through Grade 12—more than one million in the United States, by one estimate—taking online courses. [15]

More of such plagiarism—across the curriculum and in general education courses—is also the future of education. Once again, technology seems to prove that the downsides of something—anything—are about equal in depth and intensity to the benefits of that thing. And while the idea of tailoring an education to each student sounds good, it raises new risks, too. If students take for granted that they deserve an education experience customized to them, then if they don't like the experience, they are free to reject it . . . like skipping around on an iPod.

Technology also complicates our understanding of education and schools in another, perhaps surprising, way. Buildings are a kind of technology, too, and school staff have long intuitively sensed that new buildings will cause a bump in student performance, at least for a time. Indeed, James Rydeen reviewed a variety of studies that found a connection between the physical environment of a school and student performance. [16]

Rydeen summarized several studies showing higher performance in nicer buildings, though, he pointed out, some of the studies don't appear to have clearly enough separated the coincidence of socio-economic factors from building quality, or to have shown causality. The studies do posit and find that nicer buildings generate better test scores. It seems plausible, then, that teachers' intuition that their own excitement about a new building will transfer to students, who will then perform a little bit better, bears some legitimacy. It remains unclear how long this bump will last, though. [17]

Does this mean that physical infrastructure needs to undergo substantial renovation much more routinely than is typically the case? If test score improvement is really the best measure of success in education, would best practice require continual building, or at least rebuilding, of schools? The questions are farcical, but they make one of the points put forward in this book. We make tradeoffs in the decision making about everything, including education, and claims to something called best practice must take account of what values we prefer to pursue over others.

Educators, reformers, and policy makers offer bold claims about what technology can do for education. Too often, the seemingly innocuous claims—like the one about the changed nature of writing—are dangerous. Such brazenness invokes the risk of diminishing the seriousness of our approach to issues.

While digital realities are important, the increasing digitization of reading and writing (and the greater variety and brevity of material that people read and write) also affects the neural wiring of the brain, which then establishes/ affects the prospects and constraints for further reading and writing activity. But claiming that digitization has changed the nature of writing, when it hasn't, raises the prospect that we miss or diminish this other actually serious situation.

Brazen claims get attention, though. It's easier to get on TV or make a blogging name for yourself with attention-getting statements. Imagine, if possible, reframing the story. "Some teachers have used digital tools to try to stimulate more enthusiasm for writing. There are benefits as well as costs to doing this. Overall, some teachers have found it somewhat helpful." This wouldn't grab the attention of readers (increasingly in need of the dramatic, since it's more entertaining), even though it's more accurate.

Technology can indeed create certain educational benefits, but we need to be clear about the narrow range of what those benefits—and their real prospects—are. An entertainment model of education is treacherous, and social media engagement is risky. Adapting education to individual student needs is more promising, but also complicated. In short, technology adds educational value, but increases organizational complexity at the same time. Not only do technologies themselves have failures, they bind the organizational working parts of school more tightly together, thereby creating more opportunities and higher potential for normal accidents in education.

NOTES

1. PBS News Hour Online Forum, January 17, 1996, "Neil Postman Ponders High Tech," http://www.pbs.org/newshour/forum/january96/postman_1-17.html.

2. Kevin Forgarty, "Tech Predictions Gone Wrong," *ComputerWorld*, October 22, 2012. http://www.computerworld.com/s/article/9232610/Tech_predictions_gone_wrong.

3. The Economist Online, "I'm a Lumberjack," *The Economist*, April 3, 2012. http://www.economist.com/blogs/graphicdetail/2012/04/daily-chart-0.

4. LaMond Beatty, *The Instructional Media Library* (Englewood Cliffs, NJ: Educational Technology Publications, 1981), 4.

5. Reading material linked at this class room web site—http://www.steilacoom.k12.wa.us//Domain/131-—can be tracked, for instance, by number of hits. Monitoring the rate of students accessing the reading routinely revealed that much less than half the students opened or downloaded that particular day's material.

6. Annie Murphy Paul, "Likely to Succeed Amanda Ripley's 'Smartest Kids in the World,' " *The New York Times*, August 22, 2103. http://www.nytimes.com/2013/08/25/books/review/amanda-ripleys-smartest-kids-in-the-world.html?pagewanted=all&_r=0.

7. Matt Richtel, "A Silicon Valley School That Doesn't Compute." *New York Times*, October 22, 2011. http://www.nytimes.com/2011/10/23/technology/at-waldorf-school-in-silicon-valley-technology-can-wait.html.

8. Laura Heitin, "Writing Re-Launched: Teaching with Digital Tools," *EdWeek*, April 4, 2011. http://www.edweek.org/tsb/articles/2011/04/04/02digital.h04.html.

9. See *New York Times* series, "Times Topics: Brains on Electronics," at http://topics.nytimes.com/top/features/timestopics/series/your_brain_on_computers/index.html.

10. Matt Richtel, "Technology Changing How Students Learn, Teachers Say," *The New York Times*, November 1, 2011. http://www.nytimes.com/2012/11/01/education/technology-is-changing-how-students-learn-teachers-say.html?pagewanted=all.

11. Debbie Caffazzo, "iPads work well for little kids in new preschools," *The News Tribune*, November 3, 2012. http://www.thenewstribune.com/2012/11/03/2354529/ipads-are-their-favorites.html.

12. Michelle Davis, "Schools Use Digital Tools to Customize Education," *Education Week*, March 17, 2011. http://www.edweek.org/ew/articles/2011/03/17/25overview.h30.html?intc=TC11EWH.

13. 9 in 5 online forum, 2013, Broadband in Schools, http://99in5.org/.

14. Survey and Attention Test activities undertaken by two eighth-grade Language Arts teachers, Pioneer Middle School, DuPont, WA, 2010.

15. Trip Gabriel, "More Pupils Are Learning Online, Fueling Debate on Quality," *The New York Times*, April 5, 2011. http://www.nytimes.com/2011/04/06/education/06online.html?_r=3&.

16. James Rydeen, "Test Case: Do new schools mean improved test scores?" *American School & University*, August 1, 2009. http://asumag.com/constructionplanning/test-case.

17. At least one school, built in 2008 and featured in 2009 *American School and University* magazine article on green schools—http://asumag.com/green/cover—soon allowed its "greenness" to slide into inconsequentiality. The teaching garden shown in one photograph became a weed patch by the time the article came out, and remained so for several years.

Chapter Eight

Markets and Education

Markets, and the logic of efficiency, are supposed to make schools better by subjecting them to a kind of discipline that the ossified school structures currently avoid. In this chapter we will see that market analogies and logic fit awkwardly in analyzing schools. We have seen how schools function as complex bureaucratic organizations prone to normal failures, so it would seem that market forces could crack the structures that schools and the school system are. We have also seen that education is a sloppy and expensive process. As such, measuring school performance by the "bottom line" metrics of business will not yield the practical and conceptual clarity that market reformers hope for.

An education analyst at the Evergreen Freedom Foundation, a think tank in Olympia, Washington, once compared education to macaroni and cheese. Essentially, she argued that in the same way we're accustomed to twenty-eight varieties of that food product, we really deserve a similar market competition in education.[1] This is, perhaps, the clearest example of the conceptual disconnect arising from thinking about schools according to market assumptions and logic.

The macaroni metaphor grossly simplifies the complex reality of education by creating a kind of rhetorical sleight of hand which is intended to make us think that market forces—specifically consumer choice—are the solution to the problems that are supposed to beset the schools. But the producing, selling, buying, and consuming of macaroni and cheese are not much like provision—let alone consumption—of education service. Market logic itself tells us so.

The dozens of macaroni options available in the store are largely interchangeable. They are packaged, sized, designed, and colored similarly, and they come in a few basic types—traditional boil and mix, microwavable tubs, and "fun-shaped" novelty noodles. Most importantly, they taste about the same (except for the one three-cheese variety and the two whole wheat options). So, though there are twenty-eight varieties, they are fundamentally similar. In fact, most of the variation is for marketing purposes. The Scooby Doo variety differs from Sponge Bob only in that it broadens the prospect of catching more children's attention. The two otherwise look, smell, and taste somewhat the same.

Unless a macaroni consumer is looking for the novelty of something like PowerPuff Girl noodles, or has brand loyalty, most macaroni purchasers are price sensitive. This means that when one similar (almost interchangeable) option is priced lower than the others, many consumers will purchase that one. Consumers can—and sometimes do—even switch brands for price (or novelty) purposes.

This, then, begins to explain how macaroni is not like schools. Macaroni is purchased and consumed. This discrete process may be repeated, but each purchase is fundamentally independent of other macaroni purchases. Purchase decisions made last week have little bearing on purchases made this week.

Not so with schools. Macaroni purchases are of much lower consequence than educational processes, in part because macaronis are not sentient beings with parents who want particular outcomes from the continuous (not discrete) production process. Switching schools—even in an environment of high school choice—could never be anywhere as easy as switching brands for an eighty-nine-cent macaroni purchase.

Perhaps this inflexibility of movement reflects the lack of options in school choice. But then again, perhaps it reflects the economies of scale problem. Achieving economies of scale means maximizing on the efficiency that comes from production in larger volumes. This side of the economic analysis is often left off by the competition advocates because it takes more account of the reality that a capital- and labor-intensive activity like education (in American education it really is both) becomes more efficient when done on a larger scale.

Lots of variety in schools (and therefore smaller schools) means smaller scale and reduced efficiency. In other words, two different strains of economic logic actually work at cross purposes in this case. It would be great to have innumerable different types of schools—and it would be cost ineffective. We can't have it both ways, wider variety and lower production price. We can't, for instance, all have individualized macaroni designs. Whoever was next in line—desiring the twenty-ninth, and yet unavailable, macaroni—will leave the market in disappointment. Here again, then, we face significant tradeoffs when thinking about our education "system," but tradeoffs too often ignored.

The issue of tradeoffs points to another conceptual difficulty in broadly applying "market logic" to education production. Namely, we lack a good metric for "efficiency" in evaluating schools or the education system. Economists let prices do a great deal of both the practical communicating and theoretical measuring in their ideas and prescriptions, but pricing education production is made difficult because "test score outcomes" are not easily monetized, so the correlation between test scores and profit (the monetary measure reflecting gains in efficiency) is merely arbitrary.

One of the most extensive studies of efficiency in schools, by the Center for American Progress (CAP), relies on precisely this arbitrary correlation, though. The study uses a combination of expenditures on schools and test scores to arrive at the operational measure of efficiency. The higher test score achievement per dollar of expenditure means a district is more efficient. Predicted efficiency is determined by the aggregate ranking of districts, which means that performance is determined by comparison among similar districts. A district would be deemed "efficient" if it gets higher pass rates per dollar than other districts of similar size. To look good—to be deemed efficient—a district just has to beat its neighbors, so to speak.

The findings based on this study generate as many questions as answers, which warrants a thorough review of the study's claims and findings. Below, the points from the CAP report are addressed immediately thereafter.

> Many school districts could boost student achievement without increasing spending if they used their money more productively. An Arizona school district, for example, could see as much as a 36 percent boost in achievement if it increased its efficiency from the lowest level to the highest, all else being equal.

What is "more productive spending"? How do we know it when we see it, other than observing success measures (scores, presumably) go up. How is efficiency defined in connection to test scores without the whole thing becoming a tautology?

We need to have an a priori definition of efficiency and productive spending, and the logic employed in the CAP analysis does not provide that. Further, rendering appropriate social choice according to the Return on Investment matrix (provided in the report) is unclear. It remains to be shown that we should necessarily say high achievement at high cost is less efficient than medium achievement at low cost, or that high achievement at medium cost is equal in efficiency to medium achievement at low cost. In the latter case, even if we accept this efficiency grading system, this gives us no guidance about the choice between the two situations.

A social or collective choice among such a variety of options will be wholly unclear. Kenneth Arrow's impossibility theorem[2] explains why. Ar-

ROI Evaluation Matrix

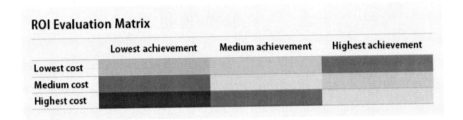

Figure 8.1.   Comparative Returns on Educational Investment. Source: Center for American Progress

row showed that the collective choice among as few as three options will not actually reflect a rationally preference ordered choice of the largest number of individuals in the group, without invoking some form of authority to shape or mandate the choice. (Voting procedures are the most obvious example of shaping outcomes.)

Individual preference orderings don't always coherently transfer to collective choice. Arrow showed this for choices among three candidates in an election. Imagine how much harder the collective choosing process is when dealing with much larger option sets that create much more complicated tradeoffs among them.

This tradeoff difficulty arises routinely when it comes to something as mundane as scheduling (master school schedule and student schedule, both). School staff individually prefer different things (planning time with their grade-level colleagues vs. planning with subject area colleagues—in middle and high school; more professional development on whole school issues like discipline vs. grade or subject area training) that must be reconciled into a collective choice for the whole staff. Even if this decision process was governed by "what's best" for students, logic and evidence are available to support divergent options.

Since student needs and preferences vary widely, no immediately clear "best practice" emerges, and since the culture of education values inclusiveness and honoring of the stakeholders' preferences, the collective choosing becomes a process of trying to satisfy as many people as possible. Obviously, what works effectively for some students (and staff) won't work as well for others. Group 2 may need or want something that turns out to be detrimental to group 3, whose dominant need actually undermines group 1 . . . and a little leadership must assert some measure of authority over the situation.

Low productivity costs the nation's school system as much as $175 billion a year. This figure is an estimate; our study does not capture everything that goes into creating an efficient district. But the approximate loss in capacity equals about 1 percent of the nation's gross domestic product.

Again, what is efficient? And how do schools achieve greater efficiency? The report does point to administrative costs as a driver of inefficiency. If pursuit of efficiency means things like cutting the excess principals in a building, that can be problematic. To lose one principal can make a school much less productive. Discipline management, for instance, is less clear and cohesive, and that intrudes into every aspect of the school day.

Talk of productivity disruptions is meaningless if we don't know how to quantify them. And of course, if you simply want the best test scores for the least spending, you need to figure out how to get rid of the low-performing students. They're a horrible drag on efficiency. The struggling learners take up a lot more time and attention than the students who are on grade level.

Without controls on how additional school dollars are spent, more education spending will not automatically improve student outcomes. In more than half of the states included in our study, there was no clear relationship between spending and achievement after adjusting for other variables, such as cost of living and students in poverty. These findings are consistent with existing research: How a school system spends its dollars can be just as important as how much it spends, at least above some threshold level.

Lacking a clear relationship between spending and achievement? Is it wise, then, to make this relationship the definition of efficiency? More spending will not automatically improve outcomes, at least above some threshold level. Market logicians should not be surprised by this; it's called diminishing marginal returns, and that does apply here. These are not particularly stunning claims, in other words. Somewhat unresolved, however, is clarity about how schools should spend their money—what will "controls" look like? More on that later.

Efficiency varies widely within states. Some districts spent thousands more per student to obtain the same broad level of academic achievement. After adjusting for factors outside of a district's control, the range of spending among the districts scoring in the top third of achievement in California was nearly $8,000 per student.

"Factors outside the district's control" can be huge, and those factors have an interactive effect that distorts results. A district with more involved parents who tell and show their children that education is important will have some ability to spend less per student and still get good test scores. Districts—or schools—that have less parent involvement will tend to do worse. Schools and districts have shown some gains for low-performing students by providing programs that make up for the consequences of reduced parent involvement.

Such programs will reduce these schools' efficiency, though. In other words, the schools where students perform poorly are precisely the ones that will require extra resources with which to help the struggling students, thereby reducing that school's efficiency even further. Pouring extra resources—say, more early education programs in the neighborhoods where parents tend toward less involvement in their children's education—into low-scoring students can help them substantially, but since those kids are on low side of the test score spectrum, it may not raise a school's test pass rate. Again, the measure of performance and improvement that we use will have substantial effect on a school's assessment.

One factor that has a lot to do with success is level of parent involvement and general family stability. A district with highly engaged and involved parents can call less upon the school to do so much of the educating, thereby increasing that school's "efficiency." Defining efficiency in the way the CAP report does, in other words, sets up a vicious circle in which schools can register as "inefficient" because their students need the school to replace what less involved parents didn't provide.

> More than a million students are enrolled in highly inefficient districts. Over 400 school districts around the country were rated highly inefficient on all three of our productivity metrics. These districts serve about 3 percent of the almost 43 million students covered by our study.

And, at the same time, the Alliance for Excellent Education reports the following:

> Approximately two thousand high schools (about 12 percent of American high schools) produce more than half of the nation's dropouts. In these dropout factories, the number of seniors enrolled is routinely 60 percent or less than the number of freshmen three years earlier.
>
> Eighty percent of the high schools that produce the most dropouts can be found in a subset of just fifteen states. The majority of dropout factories are located in northern and western cities and throughout the southern states. [3]

Unless those 2,000 high schools are all from those 400 districts, efficiency and retention may not be highly correlated. So, which do we, as a society, focus on? Or, to say it differently, how do we increase efficiency and retain students at the same time?

> High-spending school systems are often inefficient. Our analysis showed that after accounting for factors outside of a district's control, many high spending districts posted middling productivity results. For example, only 17 percent of

Florida's districts in the top third in spending were also in the top third in achievement.

This is true, by definition. When spending goes up, or test success goes down, it necessarily reduces a school's or district's efficiency. Furthermore—again, which outside factors are they referring to? If those high-spending districts were paying for mandated programs to some target population, they may not be able to get out from underneath that spending requirement. A district with a high volume of special needs students is going to be much less efficient, whatever way you define it.

Students from disadvantaged backgrounds are more likely to be enrolled in highly inefficient districts. Students who participated in subsidized lunch programs were 12 percentage points more likely to be enrolled in the nation's least-productive districts, even after making allowances for the higher cost of educating lower-income students.

This is no surprise, given the way the study defines efficiency. In this case, low-scoring students are the issue, not lower-income students. Since low socio-economic status correlates with lower parent involvement, lower reading success at early grades, lower test scores, and so forth, then those districts will have to participate in more special programs designed to support lower-scoring students, and will be less efficient.

Further, kids who fall behind early will require remediation, and while those programs achieve their curricular goals, without reinforcement and persistence outside of school, the gains are diminished and the student remains somewhat behind, thus requiring more support, and so on. In other words, the need for extra support tends to be ongoing, not once-for-all.

Highly productive districts are focused on improving student outcomes. We surveyed a sample of highly productive districts to learn more about their principles and practices. The districts that performed well on our metrics shared a number of values and practices, including strong community support and a willingness to make tough choices.

This bit is nonsensical. A good district focuses on student outcomes and "performed" well on strong community support. This implicitly acknowledges that community/parent involvement is a boon to a school. Of course, in great degree, community support is up to the members of the community, not the school.

States and districts fail to evaluate the productivity of schools and districts. While the nation spends billions of dollars on education, only two states, Florida and Texas, currently provide annual school-level productivity evaluations, which report to the public how well funds are being spent at the local level.

The quality of state and local education data is often poor. In many instances, key information on school spending and outcomes is not available or insufficiently rigorous, and this severely impedes the study of educational productivity. For instance, we did not have good enough data to control for certain cost factors, such as transportation. So a rural district with high busing costs might suffer in some of our metrics compared with a more densely populated district.

The nation's least-productive districts spend more on administration. The most inefficient districts in the country devote an extra 3 percentage points of their budgets on average to administration, operations, and other noninstructional expenditures.

Some urban districts are far more productive than others. While our main results are limited to within-state comparisons, we were able to conduct a special cross-state analysis of urban districts that recently participated in a national achievement test. After adjusting for certain factors outside a district's control, we found that some big-city school systems spend millions of dollars more than others—but get far lower results on math and reading tests.

All this is not to say that the idea of greater competition and wider variety would be a bad thing. Competition may be salutary, but achieving the benefits of competition will be much more complicated, and take more creativity and thought than buying macaroni. This is so because markets do not solve every problem in education. In production of consumer goods, the appeal of market logic is compelling. We all enjoy the wider availability of good things at low prices because of markets.

Along the way, though, we choose moral balances between efficiency and other good things we value. Labor laws protect children, and industrial laws protect adults, for instance. These are choices we make in political society. The market wouldn't "care" (since it lacks the kind of agency required to make moral choices) whether a child were put into dangerous working conditions, but people can and do care about just such things. Likewise, they care about their children's education.

The point here is that the claims of market supporters are well founded—efficiency gains, maximization of production at lower prices, and so on. But the collective choices we make about education have a social and moral, so to speak, component. Markets may improve schools and education in certain ways, but they are just as likely to weaken or subvert in other ways.

Ironically, Bill Gates's Microsoft reveals just this mixed bag, and serves as something of a cautionary tale regarding our assumptions that "market forces" will necessarily produce better outcomes in school. Microsoft—or more precisely, understanding the discussion about Microsoft—is vexing. By turns you can find claims about Microsoft's irrelevance,[4] then the secret of

Microsoft's success,[5] and gushing reports of how much money Microsoft makes.[6]

This divergence may derive from different sensibilities and loyalties about Microsoft, and differing views of what Microsoft is and does. People in the computing world argue over whether Microsoft creates anything worth using, while business people focus more on how much money the company makes. It is, of course, possible that Microsoft could make dull products while making enormous amounts of money on them. Of course, computer people and business people respond very differently to the idea that Microsoft's revenue-earning capacity may have derived less from its creating useful and innovative products than its dominance in parts of the operating system and software markets.

In other words, Microsoft's success, when measured as revenue and profit, is easily determined and compared to others—like Apple and Google. Indeed, an investor in Microsoft would want returns, whether by its constantly turning out new, effective, cool, hip (whatever) products, or by market dominance with old, uncool, stodgy products—it wouldn't necessarily matter, especially in the short run.

By contrast, evaluating Microsoft's success in terms of quality and usefulness of products involves much more subjective analyses. For instance, Microsoft's phenomenal success stems from massive sales of relatively few specific products. Apple, by contrast, generates less revenue, and less profit per dollar of revenue, but they sell a wider variety of products that generate astoundingly enthusiastic loyalty from customers.

So how should we measure and evaluate the comparative success of Microsoft and Apple? Two metrics of success yield very different conclusions about the two companies. Further, markets and competition also look different over time. Some players win and advance, while others slip back—then it flips. Further, while companies compete in the market, they also rent-seek[7]—pursue economic advantage in the political arena.

Firms of even modest size do some of both. We have no reason to think it would be any different with schools operating in a climate of "market forces"—measures of performance will remain variable and debatable, political arguments about what we should value will persist, and performance, however it's measured, will vary over time. A brief review of the charter and voucher school experience shows just this.

More than ten years ago, the Rand Corporation issued several recommendations, following on a study of vouchers (financial subsidies that allow families to pick a private school) and charter schools (publicly funded schools that operate outside the regular bureaucratic structure of the school system). One of the report's[8] (three) suggestions is particularly germane to the points being made in this book:

To ensure that voucher and charter programs benefit the students who remain in conventional public schools, policymakers should require that all participating schools practice open admissions to prevent "cream skimming" of the best students into elite schools. They should also encourage the performance of conventional public schools by giving them the autonomy they need to perform in a newly competitive educational market.

Drawing the best students (who tend to come from the more involved parents) and refusing or dismissing poorer students has long been a pervasive concern about charters and vouchers. One story about private schools in New York reveals private school leaders indulging in euphemistic language that fools no one. One school head revealed that there were "some kids that we're not going to renew"—reflecting that the school has authority over the decision about whom it will keep, which typical public schools do not. Schools dismiss those underperforming students by a process called "counseling out."[9]

Unless rules are written to prevent it, charter schools, having an extraordinary appeal, are even able to select students who will be allowed in to begin with. Though schools and districts have developed varying selection procedures, they all focus on or emphasize the selection of better students over poorer students, and the school ends up with a student body arbitrarily constituted of good students. Vouchers are subject to the same problem, as they may be applied to the tuition for private schools, precisely the places where this "counseling out" occurs.

Even random lotteries of enrollment slots do not necessarily correct for the skewing of access toward the better students. Where lottery participation is based on self-selection, more involved and engaged parents will be more likely than the less engaged parents—who tend to have the lower-performing students, on average—to invest the time and effort involved in the lottery process. Further, once in, underperforming students are still subject to "counseling out."

The second sentence in the Rand recommendation—"They should also encourage the performance of conventional public schools by giving them the autonomy they need to perform in a newly competitive educational market"—is also important. Conventional public schools that are left to compete with the charter and voucher schools need the autonomy to do so. The first seven chapters of this book have done nothing if not demonstrate that external control over schools has been increasing, and with it diminishes the likelihood of such autonomy being granted.

Rand's recommendations and guidelines maintain their relevance today. So, too, does the rather understated observation, which could serve as something of a thesis statement for both the Rand report and this book: "Some tradeoffs between desired outcomes may be necessary." We know these recommendations and this observation remain true, because the current experience with vouchers and charters shows it.

One recommendation Rand most assuredly did not make was to politicize the issue of vouchers and charters, but this happens all too much. A New York City voucher experiment, for instance, has stirred up intense academic heat, if not educational light. In the late 1990s, low-income families were randomly selected to receive a private school voucher, if they would like it. In 2012, Chingos and Peterson reviewed the college enrollment rates for voucher winners, both those who actually used the voucher and those who didn't. Their analysis revealed what they claim was a significant effect for African Americans.

> A voucher offer is shown to have increased the overall (part-time and full-time) enrollment rate of African Americans by 7.1 percentage points, an increase of 20 percent. If the offered scholarship was actually used to attend private school, the impact on African American college enrollment is estimated to be 8.7 percentage points, a 24 percent increase.[10]

Sara Goldbrick-Rab challenged the statistical validity of the study. She further diminishes the robustness of the findings by pointing out that the authors fail to address the absence of "evidence that the vouchers were effective in advancing the participation of students in higher education."[11] In other words, she says they fail to substantiate that vouchers were the causal mechanism in the increased college participation.

Indeed, it seems that merely being offered, though not using, a voucher increased African American college participation nearly as much (7.1 percentage points) as scholarships actually used (8.7 percentage points). A wide-ranging and important research program awaits anyone intent on figuring out why the mere offer of a scholarship had such a salutary effect on college participation, but for now we can only acknowledge that these findings imply that if we want to increase African American college enrollment, we need only offer—but not grant—school vouchers.

Herein lies the political aspect of the issue. As *Inside Higher Ed*[12] noted in reviewing this debate, enthusiasm for vouchers is primarily the domain of Republicans. By contrast, Chingos and Peterson argue that Democrats remain in the clutches of teachers unions that continue to resist the educational good news of vouchers. Along the way, arguments over how to understand the data are politicized. For some reason, though, such ideological battles never besmirch the fervent commitment to using data for understanding everything about students, teachers, and the performance of both.

Plenty of other efforts with vouchers have been made around the country, most with mixed result, which only fans the political flames of debate. In the mid-2000s, Florida tried a Corporate Tax Credit Scholarship program for private schools. Initial test results were not very promising. The first report of the program's results revealed, "The mean reading gain for program participants [was] -0.1 national percentile ranking points in reading and -0.9 national percentile ranking points in mathematics."[13] In the report's conclusion, the program director acknowledged that these gains were "comparable in magnitude, if perhaps modestly smaller, [to the] gains in the public school comparison groups."[14]

Washington, DC, did a voucher lottery in the mid-2000s, as well. Starting in 2004, students were randomly drawn from the list of eligible applicants to receive a grant to attend a private school. In 2009, the program was evaluated. High school graduation rates showed significant improvement—jumping 12 percentage points.[15] SAT reading and math scores showed negligible change, though.

The vouchered student average reading SAT was 649.15, while the control group was 645.24—a difference of less than 4 points. The difference in math even less, 0.7 of a point.[16] These data were not without controversy, of course. Paul Peterson, supporter of the New York vouchers, defended the gains as more significant than "reporting rules" allowed the study authors to say.[17]

Another study finds that vouchers help students achieve at higher levels, but acknowledges that it remains unclear what would happen, in the psychology of students, if everybody were getting the vouchers. In other words, student motivation and commitment may increase—thereby increasing performance—as a result of the "special" status attendant in a voucher. The special status might diminish if all students had them.[18] This study also fell back on the timeless caveat offered in so much social science scholarship, calling for more research into the issue.

More research, however, will not likely settle what really is a political or ideological issue. Kenneth Arrow may help us understand this. Since personal and public views and values about education vary so widely, no particular institutional arrangement—voucher, charter, public, home school—will meet every individual preference. The specific results of any number of studies can be deployed to bolster whichever preference you choose, but as those results tend toward a narrow focus on particular outcome measures, the claims they are supposed to support can still be countered or refuted from other diverging preferences.

Ultimately, this leaves markets, vouchers, and charters as unsatisfying means to improve education. To embrace vouchers and charters is to stimulate more organizational and regulatory complexity. Doing so, the marginal benefits of these market-oriented instruments would probably just about match the consequences of the increased likelihood of normal accidents in education.

NOTES

1. Marsha Michaelis, "Our schools deserve at least as many choices as our grocery stores," *The Port Orchard Independent*, January 27, 2011. http://www.portorchardindependent.com/opinion/114750269.html.

2. The Concise Encyclopedia of Economics, "Kenneth Arrow." http://www.econlib.org/library/Enc/bios/Arrow.html.

3. The All4Ed Graduation Rate Fact Sheet at http://www.all4ed.org/files/GraduationRates_FactSheet.pdf has since been removed.

4. Zach Epstein, "The 'irrelevance of Microsoft' illustrated in a single chart," *BGR News*, July 22, 2013. http://news.yahoo.com/irrelevance-microsoft-illustrated-single-chart-161056360.html.

5. Greg Satell, "The Secret of Microsoft's Success (And Some Lessons For Apple)," *Forbes*, April 15, 2013. http://www.forbes.com/sites/gregsatell/2013/04/15/the-secret-of-microsofts-success-and-some-lessons-for-apple/.

6. "The money made by Microsoft, Apple and Google, 1985 until today," *Royal Pingdom* (blog), April 9, 2010, http://royal.pingdom.com/2010/04/09/the-money-made-by-microsoft-apple-and-google-1985-until-today/.

7. David Henderson, *The Concise Encyclopedia of Economics*, "Rent Seeking." Accessed August 12, 2013. http://www.econlib.org/library/Enc/RentSeeking.html.

8. Brian Gill et al., *What Do We Know About Vouchers and Charter Schools? Separating the Rhetoric from the Reality* (Working paper, Rand Corporation, 2001), http://www.rand.org/pubs/research_briefs/RB8018/index1.html.

9. Sarah Maslin Nir, "Private Schools 'Counsel Out' the Unsuccessful," *The New York Times*, January 5, 2011. http://www.nytimes.com/2011/01/06/nyregion/06private.html?_r=1&.

10. Matthew Chingos, and Paul Peterson, *The Effects of School Vouchers on College Enrollment: Experimental Evidence from New York City* (Working paper, Brown Center on Education Policy at Brookings Institution, 2012), www.brookings.edu/~/media/Research/Files/Papers/2012/8/23/Impacts_of_School_Vouchers_FINAL.pdf, p. iv.

11. Sara Goldbrick-Rab, *Review of the Effects of School Vouchers on College Enrollment: Experimental Evidence from New York City* (Working paper, National Education Policy Center, 2012), http://nepc.colorado.edu/thinktank/review-vouchers-college, p. 7.

12. Doug Lederman, "Higher Ed Scholars' Voucher War," *Inside Higher Ed*, September 13, 2012. www.insidehighered.com/news/2012/09/13/researchers-argue-over-school-vouchers-impact-college-going.

13. David Figlio, *Evaluation of Florida's Corporate Tax Credit Scholarship Program First Follow-Up Report — Participation, Compliance and Test Scores in 2007-08* (Working paper, University of Florida, 2009), http://www.floridaschoolchoice.org/information/ctc/files/figlio_report_2009.pdf. p. 2.

14. Ibid., p 47.

15. Paul Peterson, "School Vouchers in DC Produce Gains in Both Test Scores and Graduation Rates," *Education Next* (2010), http://educationnext.org/school-vouchers-in-dc-produce-gains-in-both-test-scores-and-graduation-rates/, p. xi.

16. Ibid.

17. Ibid.

18. Patrick Wolf, "School Voucher Programs: What the Research Says About Parental School Choice," *Brigham Young University Law Review*, 2008, no. 2 (2008), 414-446.

Chapter Nine

Where We Go From Here

There are people everywhere who see something that needs to be done and start doing it, without the government's permission or advice or waiting for grants . . . they just do it.

—Wendell Berry

What now, then? What NOT to do seems clear enough (don't adopt a national curriculum, don't connect scores to teacher evaluations, don't put more kids in Head Start), but what TO DO is more vexing. In general, more trust among all parties (parents, school staff, school leadership, and students) must be stimulated, which means more "involvement" by parents and community members in the school. If school is about relationships, we need to work on fostering better educational relationships. Several specific structural changes will help, but culture cannot be created by regulation.

Plenty of structural, organizational, and technological changes are available to address some of the problems raised throughout this book. But any change, or reform, will only be truly worthwhile insofar as it reduces regulatory complexity and/or stimulates trust among the relevant participants in the education process—namely students, and beyond that parents and staff in the local school.

In a social conversation that marginalizes local participants, though, changes to education need to clearly produce greater access to and involvement at the local level. Only since the advent of modern bureaucratized states has a distant and amorphous education "structure" grown up that has effectively supplanted parents and community members. Education reform that neglects to address—indeed, reverse—this trend will only be more noise in an already cacophonous system.

Scholars and practitioners from the burgeoning field of decision science understand the value of local input to important social and regulatory issues. In the last several years, in applied areas such as environmental policy, so-called structured decision making has gathered increasing momentum among policy makers and institutions responsible for implementing policy. The key element of such structured decisions is the inclusion of all parties involved in and subject to the issues connected to the policy problem.

The requirements for effective structured decision making include a mutual commitment of all participants to seek general agreement on the basic facts of the situation under consideration. Next, values-based claims are heard and evaluated for clarity and coherence. While all values claims are not the same, equitability of treatment for all claims (factual and values based) allows all to be considered, if not accepted.

Finally, the decision can then follow a step-by-step process in which participants can define objectives and outcome measurements, create policy alternatives, estimate the consequence of those alternatives, evaluate trade-offs inherent in policy options, and implement and monitor the best policy.

The point of the process is precisely to include other, particularly local, voices because all too often "local knowledge is uncritically rejected because it is viewed by science-dominated processes as insufficiently objective . . . and rigorous."[1] The previous eight chapters of this book have demonstrated that such rejection or dismissal holds true in education, as national and state experts, bureaucrats, and reformers claim title to the necessary specialized information and knowledge (indeed, they create the very information—test scores and their analysis, for instance—they deem worthy of inclusion in the discussion) that grants access to the conversation.

In short, the increasing regulation of education, the rising centralization of authority over schools, and the greater distance between governing bodies and classrooms makes for a decision environment in need of some restructuring.

Local involvement is, of course, still available in education and schools. But such involvement tends toward either very specific parental concerns about a child, or marginal issues about relatively inconsequential procedure. The more substantive issues about testing, standards, or curriculum are typically far removed (geographically and socially) from parents or other local actors. The "experts" have handed down standardized tests and the Common Core, for instance, and the local discussion may involve either distaste (rather futile distaste, at that) for such mandates, or concerns about whether a school or teacher is doing enough to meet the standards.

More effective local involvement would include parent and local group participation in a consideration of what their schools need to do in order to support students' educational performance. Given the idiosyncratic nature of schools, these discussions and decisions really need to be on a school-by-school basis, and shaped around conversations among staff and parents. Too much, though, school staff must be Janus-faced, turning one way to serve students and parents, while turning the other direction to keep an eye toward checking on what the organizational masters of the education system expect from the school and its teachers.

One could not create an exhaustive list of the possible changes a particular school or district could or should consider, since individual schools and districts can be so different from each other. The conversation must, therefore, be local, as that is the best place to consider the tradeoffs peculiar to that situation. Differences in socio-economics, race, immigrant status, parental education status, and so forth, are important—and typical—demographic factors that can vary widely.

Such demographic variation extends beyond those categories already imagined by the education bureaucracy. For instance, schools with a high proportion of students from military families will have the overlay of an additional set of factors that substantially affect the educational lives of those students. The point is that individual schools face a wide range of potential concerns they must address, and to address them well, they need some degree of decision-making autonomy at the local level.

That being said, plenty of interesting and useful ideas are available as starting points in local conversations about education and schools. First, if there are structural or organizational changes that could create better education without deep philosophical change to the schools, those should be pursued most aggressively. Pick the low-hanging fruit first. Take the summer drop-off (educational performance that slips because of inactivity during the summer), for example. It is a significant problem, and the best response is to run school longer.

With a little creativity, a longer school year can be accomplished without adding to the 180 days of the teachers' contracts. Establish a calendar of forty five-day weeks for students, reserving Fridays for enrichment, special projects and activities, extra remediation, and so on and staffed by half the teachers. In other words, the teaching (and, perhaps administrative and classified) staff works nine out of every ten days, with every other Friday off.

Cancel the in-service days, stop the numerous days off that only schools take, and so on. Make necessary adjustments for the normal holidays, and a school or district could get two hundred school days for a little bit more operating expense. Students would get more instruction time, less vacation-related loss, and more time for enrichment activities, or class schedule variation.

The new understanding of how the brain learns and retains—discussed in chapter 2—now makes clear that shorter class days could also improve performance, if the schedule is managed well. This is particularly helpful for another scheduling alternative—later start times for high schools. Teenagers' biorhythms dictate that they wake up (and go to sleep) later than the rest of us, so later start times have invariably shown benefits in student performance.

Suggesting this schedule change will inevitably generate a one-word rebuttal: "buses." Again, commitment and creativity can overcome this. For instance, younger children are typically awake much earlier than their 9 AM school start time, so switching elementary and high school start times is the place to begin the discussion.

Another structural change that schools and local discussants might consider is ability grouping. The once common, then renounced, practice is making a comeback. Perhaps this philosophical reversal reflects pedagogical incoherence, but more likely it indicates the fact that different schools and communities have different needs. Indeed, a *New York Times* article covering the growing phenomenon undertook the necessary journalistic effort to consider what the research says about grouping. Unfortunately, doing so creates more confusion than clarity:

> Some studies indicate that grouping can damage students' self-esteem by consigning them to lower-tier groups; others suggest that it produces the opposite effect by ensuring that more advanced students do not make their less advanced peers feel inadequate. Some studies conclude that grouping improves test scores in students of all levels, others that it helps high-achieving students while harming low-achieving ones, and still others say that it has little effect. [2]

Where do responsible school administrators, parents, and teachers go from here? They engage in serious conversation, with trust in each other, about the best route for their school to take. In the nature of our social climate around education, however, a decision such as whether to group is all too often left to higher—more remote—authorities.

Another choice for local decision makers to consider is same-sex classrooms. Ask a teacher (especially middle school) you know, and chances are that they'd be willing to give same-sex classes a try. No American experiments (at least not ones involving random selection of students, and no opt-out of the study—same-sex—group) have been conducted on this, but evidence from South Korea shows that boys and girls perform better (higher proportion go to college) in same-sex classes. [3]

Thirty-nine states and the District of Columbia offer same-sex classes, and Congress has clarified that the federal government accepts the practice. But states have final authority over this, and in an effort to preserve gender equality, Washington state (for one) has banned them. So when a struggling middle school tried it—with some success—they were told to stop. [4] This serves as a remarkably clear example of social tradeoffs we make in education (one vision of gender equality is preferred over better educational outcomes), and of the way distant actors decide things that local education participants must simply accept.

The standardized test and teacher evaluation process could also undergo some revamping, especially since increasing local participation in these issues necessitates that state and federal authorities will have stepped back some. Allowing schools and districts to implement assessments—of teachers and students—from a menu of options would be one way for state authorities to step back.

Students everywhere are already extensively assessed, so a student could earn "adequate" academic growth results from the outcomes on, say, two out of three assessments, or on some other combination of results, as chosen by the local education stakeholders. High schoolers, for instance, could be assessed on the range of subjects (from math to art) they take during their career, then deemed "proficient" or "ready to graduate" if they pass four of six or five of eight assessments (or whatever mix the district, or state for that matter, chooses).

Similarly, teachers can be evaluated according to the goals and performance their community most values when that community has local authority over the creation of the evaluation components and measures. If one community chooses to measure student success (and thereby maintains different expectations of teachers) according to different items from the assessment menu, then that community can work closely with its teachers to implement that.

In a social climate accustomed to regulation and growing national authority over education, this emphasis on local control probably seems improbable at best, undesirable in the extreme. Each of these prospective changes really only amounts to some structural adjusting, but will require a change in the culture of our conversations about schools. That is the difficult part, for it is not only teachers (and their unions) who "resist" the supposedly important reforms that will revitalize education. Nearly everyone who is entrenched in the routines that have developed around school as we've come to know it will resist.

When buses, after-school sports, student jobs, kids' need to "have fun," and summer vacation expectations are invoked in response to calls for useful and substantive changes, we are all culpable for the inertia that results, for each one of those, no matter how legitimate, has become a trope. Invoke them, and it signals that there is nothing more to say about the issue. And schools then remain the bureaucratic organization that they are.

Schools and school districts are organizations. That means they run according to a set of patterns based, ideally, on principles that will make the organization effective in pursuit of its goals, in this case, educating children. Of course, no organization executes perfectly, let alone even creates the patterns of conduct that allow ideal pursuit of the goals. Schools are no different in this way. But organizations, like people, can learn. Indeed, so-called organizational learning is much discussed in academic and business circles.

Not surprisingly, the characteristics of learning organizations read like the requirements for high-trust local decision making in schools. Learning organizations share information widely, encourage organization members to take responsibility for each other's success, respect diversity, and make interactions collaborative.[5] These may sound a bit cliché, but doing them right does require engaged participation, done in trusting and trustworthy ways.

The degree to which a school can learn, then, will affect the quality and character of that school. More personal involvement, more collaboration, more trust, and a better school will result. No amount of state or federal programs, regulations, or mandates will ever replace or transcend that. Neither will federally funded "involvement centers."

Grassroots participation has to grow from the ground up, so if you're a parent reading this, get and/or stay involved—first, in your child's school work, then in the school as an organization. Of course, if you're reading this book, you're probably already involved, so help one of your child's friend's parents get involved, or offer to help the staff at your child's school, or do some tutoring for students who need support.

If you are a teacher reading this book, make ways for parents to get and stay involved. Be patient while you develop trust and rapport each year. Communicate with parents. Take responsibility for their children's success. And take responsibility for your colleagues' success.

If you are an education bureaucrat or reformer, be a servant leader. Find ways to raise the local discussion about schools by valuing parents' and school staffs' input about their own schools. Respect the fact that they know things—even some things you don't know—about their schools and their students.

Obviously, the very highest level of the bureaucracy needs to change its thinking and expectations in order to do this, but until that happens, take personal responsibility by releasing some of the (misplaced) authorities you have over schools. Work to find ways for them to succeed, not only on the terms mandated from the hierarchy above you, but also in the ways that matter to the families and students you serve.

In this way, we might be able to reduce some of the complexity and tightness that bedevils our education "system." Looseness may be awkward to cope with, but it is what allows committed educators—parents and teachers alike—to truly do what is best for students.

NOTES

1. L. Failing, R. Gregory, and M. Harstone, "Integrating science and local knowledge in environmental risk management: A decision-focused approach," *Ecological Economics*, 64 (2007), p. 48.

2. Vivian Yee, "Grouping Students by Ability Regains Favor in Classroom," *The New York Times*, June 9, 2013. http://www.nytimes.com/2013/06/10/education/grouping-students-by-ability-regains-favor-with-educators.html?pagewanted=all&_r=1&.

3. National Association for Single Sex Public Education, "Single-Sex vs. Coed: The Evidence." http://www.singlesexschools.org/research-brain.htm.

4. Peter Callaghan, "Same-Sex Classrooms About Achievement, Not Overreaching Laws," *The News Tribune*, September 8, 2011. http://www.thenewstribune.com/2011/09/08/1814068/same-sex-classes-about-achievement.html.

5. Karen Cator, "Fire Up Teams by Creating Opportunities to Learn," July 15, 2013, http://www.linkedin.com/today/post/article/20130715184409-2906843-fire-up-teams-by-creating-opportunities-to-learn?trk=tod-home-art-list-small_1.

Bibliography

Baer, Justin, Michaela Gulemetova, and Cynthia Prince. "Research Guidance to State Affiliates on Value-Added Teacher Evaluation Systems." Working paper. National Education Association, vibrantschoolstacoma.org/wp-content/uploads/2011/07/NEA-VAM-best-practices-guide.pdf.

Beatty, LaMond. *The Instructional Media Library*. Englewood Cliffs, NJ: Educational Technology Publications, 1981.

Brice Heath, Shirley. "What No Bedtime Story Means: Narrative Skills at Home and School." *Language in Society* no. 1 (1982): 49-76.

"Broadband in Schools." (online forum message). *99 in 5*. 2013. http://99in5.org/ (accessed June 21, 2013).

Bronson, Po, and Ashley Merryman. *NurtureShock: New Thinking About Children*. New York: Twelve, 2009.

Brooks, David. "The Medium is the Medium." *The New York Times*, July 8, 2010. http://www.nytimes.com/2010/07/09/opinion/09brooks.html?_r=4& (accessed January 25, 2011).

Caffazzo, Debbie. "iPads work well for little kids in new preschools." *The News Tribune*, November 3, 2012. http://www.thenewstribune.com/2012/11/03/2354529/ipads-are-their-favorites.html (accessed November 3, 2012).

Caffazzo, Debbie. "Junior High Return Sought in Tacoma." *The News Tribune*, September 27, 2010. http://www.thenewstribune.com/2010/09/27/1357804/junior-high-return-sought.html (accessed September 27, 2010).

Callaghan, Peter. "Same-Sex Classrooms About Achievement, Not Overreaching Laws." *The News Tribune*, September 8, 2011. http://www.thenewstribune.com/2011/09/08/1814068/same-sex-classes-about-achievement.html (accessed July 12, 2013).

Camden, Jim, and Jonathan Brunt. "Tacoma Schools, teachers being called to Principal Gregoire's office." *The Spokesman-Review*, September 21, 2011. http://www.spokesman.com/blogs/spincontrol/2011/sep/21/tacoma-schools-teachers-being-called-principal-gregoires-office/ (accessed July 31, 2013).

Carollo, Kim. "Can Your Insulin Pump Be Hacked?" *ABC News: Medical Unit* (blog), April 10, 2012. abcnews.go.com/blogs/health/2012/04/10/can-your-insulin-pump-be-hacked/ (accessed July 31, 2013).

Cator, Karen. "Fire Up Teams by Creating Opportunities to Learn." July 15, 2013. http://www.linkedin.com/today/post/article/20130715184409-2906843-fire-up-teams-by-creating-opportunities-to-learn?trk=tod-home-art-list-small_1 (accessed August 18, 2013).

Chingos, Matthew, and Paul Peterson. *THE EFFECTS OF SCHOOL VOUCHERS ON COLLEGE ENROLLMENT: Experimental Evidence from New York City*. Working paper. Brown

Center on Education Policy at Brookings Institution, 2012. www.brookings.edu/~/media/ Research/Files/Papers/2012/8/23.

Chua, Amy. *Battle Hymn of the Tiger Mother*. New York: Penguin, 2011.

Chua, Amy. "Why Chinese Mothers are Superior." *The Wall Street Journal*, January 8, 2011. http://online.wsj.com/article/SB10001424052748704111504576059713528698754.html (accessed August 31, 2013).

Corrigan, Maureen. "Tiger Mothers: Raising Children the Chinese Way." *National Public Radio: Books*, January 11, 2011. http://www.npr.org/2011/01/11/132833376/tiger-mothers-raising-children-the-chinese-way (accessed July 2, 2013).

Davis, Michelle. "Schools Use Digital Tools to Customize Education." *Education Week*, March 17, 2011. http://www.edweek.org/ew/articles/2011/03/17/25overview.h30.html?intc= TC11EWH (accessed March 21, 2013).

"English Language Arts Standards » Reading: Informational Text » Grade 8." *Common Core State Standards Initiative* (blog), http://www.corestandards.org/ELA-Literacy/RI/8 (accessed August 12, 2013).

Epstein, Zach. "The 'irrelevance of Microsoft' illustrated in a single chart." *BGR News*, July 22, 2013. http://news.yahoo.com/irrelevance-microsoft-illustrated-single-chart-161056360. html (accessed July 23, 2013).

Failing, L., R. Gregory, and M. Harstone. "Integrating science and local knowledge in environmental risk management: A decision-focused approach." *Ecological Economics*. (2007): 47-60.

Flesch, Rudolf. *Why Johnny Can't Read — And What You Can Do About It*. New York: Harper & Row, 1955.

Figlio, David. *Evaluation of Florida's Corporate Tax Credit Scholarship Program First Follow-Up Report – Participation, Compliance and Test Scores in 2007-08*. Working paper. University of Florida, 2009. http://www.floridaschoolchoice.org/information/ctc/files/figlio_report_2009.pdf.

Florida Department of Education, "Florida School Grades." Accessed August 1, 2013. http:// schoolgrades.fldoe.org/.

Forgarty, Kevin. "Tech Predictions Gone Wrong." *ComputerWorld*, October 22, 2012. http:// www.computerworld.com/s/article/9232610/Tech_predictions_gone_wrong (accessed August 21, 2013).

Fryer, Jr., Ronald. "Information and Student Achievement: Evidence from a Cellular Phone Experiment." Working paper. Harvard University, 2013. http://scholar.harvard.edu/files/ fryer/files/million_manuscriptjune2013_0.pdf.

Gabriel, Trip. "More Pupils Are Learning Online, Fueling Debate on Quality." *The New York Times*, April 5, 2011. http://www.nytimes.com/2011/04/06/education/06online.html?_r=3& (accessed April 13, 2011).

Gates, Bill. "How teacher development could revolutionize our schools." *The Washington Post*, February 28, 2011. http://www.washingtonpost.com/wp-dyn/content/article/2011/02/27/ AR2011022702876.html?nav=hcmoduletmv (accessed November 13, 2012).

Gill, Brian, et al. *What Do We Know About Vouchers and Charter Schools? Separating the Rhetoric from the Reality*. Working paper. Rand Corporation, 2001. http://www.rand.org/ pubs/research_briefs/RB8018/index1.html.

Gladwell, Malcolm. *Outliers: The Story of Success*. New York: Little, Brown & Co., 2008.

Goldbrick-Rab, Sara. *Review of the Effects of School Vouchers on College Enrollment: Experimental Evidence from New York City*. Working paper. National Education Policy Center, 2012. http://nepc.colorado.edu/thinktank/review-vouchers-college.

Gordon Blankinship, Donna. "WA education advocates lobby for school reform." *The Seattle Times*, April 15, 2009. seattletimes.com/html/localnews/2009065462_ apwaxgreducationdollars.html (accessed March 12, 2010).

Harms, William. "Student performance improves when teachers given incentives upfront." See more at: http://news.uchicago.edu/article/2012/08/08/student-performance-improves-when-teachers-given-incentives-upfront.

Heitin, Laura. "Writing Re-Launched: Teaching with Digital Tools." *EdWeek*, April 4, 2011. http://www.edweek.org/tsb/articles/2011/04/04/02digital.h04.html (accessed April 21, 2011).

Henderson, David. *The Concise Encyclopedia of Economics*, "Rent Seeking." Accessed August 12, 2013. http://www.econlib.org/library/Enc/RentSeeking.html.

Hirsch, Jr., E.D., and Robert Pondiscio. "There's No Such Thing as a Reading Test." *The Core Knowledge Blog* (blog), June 16, 2010. http://blog.coreknowledge.org/2010/06/16/there's-no-such-thing-as-a-reading-test/ (accessed July 22, 2013).

Hoffman, Jan. "Online Bullies Pull Schools Into the Fray." *The New York Times*, June 27, 2010. http://www.nytimes.com/2010/06/28/style/28bully.html?pagewanted=all (accessed February 1, 2011).

Jackson, Camille. "Your Students Love Social Media . . . and So Can You." *Teaching Tolerance*. no. Spring (2011). http://www.tolerance.org/magazine/number-39-spring-2011/feature/your-students-love-social-media-and-so-can-you (accessed May 12, 2011).

Jackson, Thelma. *Addressing the Achievement Gap for African American Students in Tacoma Public Schools*. Manuscript, 2009. http://www.tacoma.k12.wa.us/information/departments/assessment/Achievement Gap Documents/Addressing the Achievement Gap Report.pdf.

Jacob, Brian, and Stephen Levitt. "Rotten Apples: An Investigation of the Prevalence and Predictors of Teacher Cheating." *Quarterly Journal of Economics*. no. 3 (2003): 843-78. http://sitemaker.umich.edu/bajacob/files/cheating.pdf (accessed July 31, 2013).

Jennings, Jack. *Why Have We Fallen Short and Where Do We Go From Here?* Manuscript, Center on Education Policy, 2012.

Kaiser Family Foundation, "Generation M2: Media in the Lives of 8- to 18-Year-Olds." Last modified January 20, 2010. Accessed April 21, 2010. http://kff.org/other/event/generation-m2-media-in-the-lives-of/.

Langewiesche, William. "The Lessons of Valujet 592." *The Atlantic*, March 1, 1998. http://www.theatlantic.com/magazine/archive/1998/03/the-lessons-of-valujet-592/306534/ (accessed April 3, 2013).

Lederman, Doug. "Higher Ed Scholars' Voucher War." *Inside Higher Ed*, September 13, 2012. http://www.insidehighered.com/news/2012/09/13/researchers-argue-over-school-vouchers-impact-college-going (accessed September 2, 2013).

Mann, Charles. "Homeland Insecurity." *The Atlantic*, September 2002. http://www.theatlantic.com/magazine/archive/2002/09/homeland-insecurity/302575/ (accessed August 2, 2013).

Maslin Nir, Sarah. "Private Schools 'Counsel Out' the Unsuccessful." *The New York Times*, January 5, 2011. http://www.nytimes.com/2011/01/06/nyregion/06private.html?_r=1& (accessed February 3, 2011).

McGuinn, Patrick. "Fight Club." *EDUCATIONnext*. no. 3 (2012). http://educationnext.org/fight-club/ (accessed August 12, 2013).

Medina, John. *Brain Rules: 12 Principles for Surviving and Thriving at Work, Home, and School*. Seattle: Pear Press, 2008.

Menand, Louis. "Today's Assignment." *The New Yorker*, December 17, 2012. http://www.newyorker.com/talk/comment/2012/12/17/121217taco_talk_menand (accessed December 30, 2012).

Michaelis, Marsha. "Our schools deserve at least as many choices as our grocery stores." *The Port Orchard Independent*, January 27, 2011. http://www.portorchardindependent.com/opinion/114750269.html (accessed January 30, 2011).

Mitchell, Ronald. "Regime Design Matters: Intentional oil pollution and treaty compliance." *International Organization*. no. 3 (1994): 425-58. http://rmitchel.uoregon.edu/sites/default/files/resume/articles_refereed/1994-IO.pdf (accessed July 1, 2013).

Mulvenon, Sean, Ronna Turner, and Shawn Thomas. *Techniques for Detection of Cheating on Standardized Tests using SAS®*. Working paper. University of Arkansas, Fayetteville. http://www2.sas.com/proceedings/sugi26/p257-26.pdf.

Murphy Paul, Annie. "Likely to Succeed Amanda Ripley's 'Smartest Kids in the World.'" *The New York Times*, August 22, 2103. http://www.nytimes.com/2013/08/25/books/review/amanda-ripleys-smartest-kids-in-the-world.html?pagewanted=all&_r=0 (accessed August 24, 2013).

National Assessment of Educational Progress, "The Nation's Report Card." Accessed June 12, 2013. http://nationsreportcard.gov/civics_2010/.

National Assessment of Educational Progress, "The Nation's Report Card—Sample Questions." Accessed September 22, 2013. http://nationsreportcard.gov/civics_2010/sample_quest.aspx.

National Association for Single Sex Public Education, "Single-Sex vs. Coed: The Evidence." Accessed August 8, 2013. http://www.singlesexschools.org/research-brain.htm.

National Parent Teacher Association, "National Parent Teacher Association." Accessed June 29, 2013. http://www.pta.org/.

Nauert, Rick. "Immediate Reward Hikes Student Performance." *Psych Central*, June 27, 2012. http://psychcentral.com/news/2012/06/27/immediate-reward-hikes-student-performance/40735.html (accessed June 17, 2013).

"Neil Postman Ponders High Tech." (Online forum message). *PBS News Hour Online Forum*. January 17, 1996. http://www.pbs.org/newshour/forum/january96/postman_1-17.html (accessed July 21, 2013).

Newcomb, Douglas. "Hackers take over a Prius, call for automakers to patch security holes." *MSN Autos* (blog), July 29, 2013. http://editorial.autos.msn.com/blogs/post--hackers-take-over-a-prius-call-for-automakers-to-patch-security-holes (accessed July 31, 2013).

Office of the Superintendent of Public Instruction. "Eliminating the Gaps." Accessed August 22, 2013. http://www.k12.wa.us/CISL/EliminatingtheGaps/CulturalCompetence/Research.aspx.

Office of the Superintendent of Public Instruction. "Frequently Asked Questions About State Testing." Accessed June 13, 2013. http://www.k12.wa.us/assessment/statetesting/faq.aspx.

Office of the Superintendent of Public Instruction. "OSPI-Developed Performance Assessments for the Arts." Accessed March 31, 2013. http://www.k12.wa.us/arts/PerformanceAssessments/default.aspx.

Office of the Superintendent of Public Instruction. "Washington State Report Card." Accessed August 2, 2013. http://reportcard.ospi.k12.wa.us/waslCurrent.aspx?groupLevel=District&schoolId=188&reportLevel=District&orgLinkId=188&yrs=2011-12&gradeLevelId=8&waslCategory=1&year=2011-12&chartType=1.

O'Neil, Patrick. "Complexity and Counterterrorism: Thinking About Biometrics." *Studies in Conflict & Terrorism*. no. 6 (2005): 547-566. http://www.tandfonline.com/doi/abs/10.1080/10576100591008962.

Parents Across America. "Confessions of a Bad Teacher: Buy the Book." Last modified August 15, 2013. Accessed August 18, 2013. http://parentsacrossamerica.org/confessions-bad-teacher-buy-book/.

Parents Across America. "Who We Are." Accessed March 3, 2011. http://parentsacrossamerica.org/who-we-are/ .

Pearson, Allison. "The Discipline of a Chinese Mother." *The Telegraph*, January 27, 2012. http://www.telegraph.co.uk/women/mother-tongue/familyadvice/9041280/The-discipline-of-a-Chinese-mother.html (accessed July 21, 2013).

Perrow, Charles. *Normal Accidents: Living with High-Risk Technologies*. New York: Basic Books, 1984.

Peterson, Paul. "School Vouchers in DC Produce Gains in Both Test Scores and Graduation Rates." *Education Next*. (2010). http://educationnext.org/school-vouchers-in-dc-produce-gains-in-both-test-scores-and-graduation-rates/ (accessed August 4, 2013).

Phillips, Rich. "Miami school's turnaround wins Obama's attention." *CNN*, March 4, 2011. http://www.cnn.com/2011/US/03/04/obama.miami.school/index.html (accessed April 21, 2013).

Piccard, Dick. Ohio University, "Book Review: *Normal Accidents*." Last modified April 14, 2011. Accessed September 28, 2012. http://www.ohio.edu/people/piccard/entropy/perrow.html.

Postman, Neil. "Language Education in a Knowledge Context." *Et cetera*. (1980): 25-37. http://neilpostman.org/articles/etc_37-1-postman.pdf (accessed July 21, 2013).

Primary Sources: America's Teachers on America's Schools. Manuscript. The Bill & Melinda Gates Foundation, 2010. http://www.scholastic.com/primarysources/pdfs/Scholastic_Gates_0310.pdf.

Putnam, Robert. *Bowling Alone: The Collapse and Revival of American Community.* New York: Simon & Schuster, 2001.

Ravitch, Diane. "Stephen Krashen: Our PISA Scores are Just Right." *Diane Ravitch's Blog* (blog), December 9, 2012. http://dianeravitch.net/2012/12/09/stephen-krashen-our-pisa-scores-are-just-right/ (accessed May 12, 2012).

Richtel, Matt. "Technology Changing How Students Learn, Teachers Say." *The New York Times*, November 1, 2011. http://www.nytimes.com/2012/11/01/education/technology-is-changing-how-students-learn-teachers-say.html?pagewanted=all (accessed November 2, 2011).

Richtel, Matt. "A Silicon Valley School That Doesn't Compute." *The New York Times*, October 22, 2011. http://www.nytimes.com/2011/10/23/technology/at-waldorf-school-in-silicon-valley-technology-can-wait.html (accessed October 24, 2011).

Rothstein, Richard, et al. *Problems with the use of student test scores to evaluate teachers.* Manuscript. Economic Policy Institute, 2010. http://www.epi.org/publication/bp278/.

Rydeen, James. "Test Case: Do new schools mean improved test scores?" *American School & University*, August 1, 2009. http://asumag.com/constructionplanning/test-case (accessed July 21, 2013).

Satell, Greg. "The Secret of Microsoft's Success (And Some Lessons For Apple)." *Forbes*, April 15, 2013. http://www.forbes.com/sites/gregsatell/2013/04/15/the-secret-of-microsofts-success-and-some-lessons-for-apple/ (accessed August 12, 2013).

Schilling, Sara. "Bethel school panel votes to recommend switch to middle school format." *The News Tribune*, December 17, 2010. http://www.thenewstribune.com/2010/12/17/1468619/bethel-board-seeks-change.html (accessed January 5, 2011).

Scoon Reid, Karla. "Family Engagement in Education Act Introduced in Congress." *K-12 Parents and the Public* (blog), July 17, 2013. http://blogs.edweek.org/edweek/parentsandthepublic/2013/07/family_engagement_in_education_act_introduced_in_congress.html (accessed July 19, 2013).

Shaw, Linda. "Gregoire wants just one state education agency." *The Seattle Times*, January 5, 2011. http://seattletimes.com/html/localnews/2013850318_edfunding06m.html (accessed January 6, 2011).

Sheaffer, Amanda. "Letter to Students from a Torn Teacher." *EdWeek*, April 4, 2011. http://www.edweek.org/tm/articles/2011/04/04/lettertesting.html (accessed May 11, 2013).

Slavin, Ronald, Nancy Karweit, and Barbara Wasik. *Preventing Early School Failure: Research, Policy, and Practice.* Needham Heights, MA: Allyn & Bacon, 1994.

Sparks, Sarah. "Innovation Criteria Is a Model for Feds." *Education Week*, October 26, 2011. http://www.edweek.org/ew/articles/2011/10/26/10innovation.h31.html (accessed June 30, 2013).

Start School Later. "Health, Safety and Equity in Education." Accessed July 10, 2013. http://www.startschoollater.net/index.html.

Strauss, Valerie. "Take this 1931 8th grade test (you will probably flunk)." *The Answer Sheet* (blog), November 23, 2010. http://voices.washingtonpost.com/answer-sheet/history/take-this-1931-8th-grade-gradu.html (accessed November 26, 2010).

Thaler, Richard, and Cass Sunstein. *Nudge: Improving Decisions About Health, Wealth, and Happiness.* New Haven: Yale University Press, 2008.

The Concise Encyclopedia of Economics. "Kenneth Arrow." Accessed August 12, 2013. *http://www.econlib.org/library/Enc/bios/Arrow.html.*

The Economist Online. "I'm a Lumberjack." *The Economist*, April 3, 2012. http://www.economist.com/blogs/graphicdetail/2012/04/daily-chart-0 (accessed July 21, 2013).

"The money made by Microsoft, Apple and Google, 1985 until today." *Royal Pingdom* (blog), April 9, 2010. http://royal.pingdom.com/2010/04/09/the-money-made-by-microsoft-apple-and-google-1985-until-today/ (accessed August 21, 2013).

van der Berg, Servaas. *Poverty and Education*. Manuscript. International Institute for Educational Planning, 2008. http://www.iiep.unesco.org/fileadmin/user_upload/Info_Services_ Publications/pdf/2009/EdPol10.pdf.

Vaughan, Diane. *The Challenger Launch Decision: Risky Technology, Culture, and Deviance at NASA*. Chicago: University of Chicago Press, 1996.

Vibrant Schools Tacoma Coalition. "Community Voices for Student Success." Accessed July 15, 2011. http://vibrantschoolstacoma.org/.

Vibrant Schools Tacoma Coalition. "Research." Accessed July 21, 2013. http://vibrantschoolstacoma.org/?page_id=6.

Whyte, William. *The Organization Man*. New York: Simon & Schuster, 1956.

Wolf, Patrick. "School Voucher Programs: What the Research Says About Parental School Choice." *Brigham Young University Law Review*. no. 2 (2008). 414-446 (accessed September 21, 2013).

Wong Keltner, Kim. *Tiger Babies Strike Back: How I Was Raised by a Tiger Mom but Could Not Be Turned to the Dark Side*. New York: William Morrow Paperbacks, 2013.

Yee, Vivian. "Grouping Students by Ability Regains Favor in Classroom." *The New York Times*, June 9, 2013. http://www.nytimes.com/2013/06/10/education/grouping-students-by-ability-regains-favor-with-educators.html?pagewanted=all&_r=1& (accessed September 1, 2013).